# A Very Present HELP

**MARY ANN MARTIN**

D1502582

Christian Light Publications, Inc.
Harrisonburg, VA 22802

A VERY PRESENT HELP

Christian Light Publications, Inc.,
Harrisonburg, Virginia 22802
© 2010 by Christian Light Publications, Inc.
All rights reserved. Published 2010
Printed in the United States of America

This book was originally published by the author
in 1987 and 1993 under the title *Consolation
Through a Time of Crisis.* It has been rewritten and updated
for this 2010 Christian Light Publications edition.

2nd Printing, 2011

Cover Design: David W. Miller

ISBN: 978-0-87813-689-6

# Contents

# Acknowledgments

We want to thank all our brethren, sisters, friends, relatives, neighbors, and acquaintances who remembered us with prayers, letters, cards, poems, gifts, and words of encouragement while we were going through this crisis. We didn't take the time to answer these letters during that time of suffering, but we determined to write a letter later to send to all who showed an interest in Nathan's recovery. Instead, this book materialized, born out of our sense of indebtedness to others.

The Lord taught us so much we didn't want to forget, so I wrote it down in a daily journal, which served as a source of information for this book. I didn't realize how hard it would be to relive the whole experience by writing about it, but the Holy Spirit urged me to keep on. All glory belongs to God, who gave strength, time, and memories to me when I needed them.

I'm especially grateful to my husband Lloyd who urged me on and encouraged me to complete this book and was the reliable source of wisdom I resorted to for discernment in what to write or omit.

Our oldest daughter Keturah was a great asset in enabling me to complete this book in one winter. Many times she offered to finish the day's work and urged me to write.

I owe appreciation to all our older children, who offered their suggestions or constructive criticisms concerning certain details of the story, and especially to our son Victor for drawing the pictures we used for the first edition.

Last but not least we owe a thank-you to Curtis and Kay Deel, who typed and edited the manuscript, and John Wesley Hackman, a cousin and friend of our family who showed his concern through our traumatic experiences and was a valuable asset in writing the last chapter.

— *Mary Ann Martin*

# 1.

# Shock

*And we know that all things work together for good
to them that love God, to them who are the called
according to his purpose.*
*— Romans 8:28*

*L*loyd gripped the van's steering wheel. His face reflected the shock and grief of the unplanned hour. The air was thick with crushed feelings and unspoken prayers for God's mercy on our son. Words had not yet penetrated the stillness as we rounded the curve and crossed the bridge a mile from our home.

I readjusted my unconscious son in my arms. "What happened?" My grief-stricken words were barely audible. Lloyd didn't answer immediately. Our spirits were stunned. I was sure Nathan's neck wasn't broken, so I lifted him from the bumpy van seat, ignoring the blood running down my dress. His dirty, bleeding form nestled limply in my arms.

It was Friday, May 30, 1986. The day had begun like any other day on our family farm in Jefferson County, New York.

Once the morning activities, chores, and responsibilities were finished, we had settled down for our regular time of family worship. Everyone who could read chose a verse from the Bible, and those who could not read repeated the verse from memory. We sang a few songs and then knelt to pray. After our family worship, Lloyd drove to the local farm supply store. The salesman there always paid attention to the little boys, who liked to go along with their father. The five older boys worked outside, and our two girls and I thought it would be a good time to clean the house.

At lunchtime the family was again united, as usual. We discussed going on a trip. Maybe we could visit our cousins in Canada this weekend. The corn was planted, and it wasn't time for haying yet. We let our imaginations run, all talking at the same time about what we would like to do in the next few weeks.

We knew not how our heavenly Father had perfectly planned our time for the weeks to come.

I had just settled down to do some sewing when our two oldest boys dashed in through the kitchen door. "Mom!" they called, almost in unison. "Nathan's hurt!"

Immediately I was in the kitchen, little thinking that the tablecloth I had been hemming wouldn't be finished until a month later.

"Bring him in," I ordered. Why had they left him outside if he was hurt? He'd probably pinched his finger or stubbed his toe or sustained any of those other minor injuries that are so common on a farm with seven boys. My sister had asked me several times, "Don't you worry about your boys? Farms have the highest statistics for serious injuries and deaths."

"No," I always told her. "I commit my children to God's protection." But had I been unconsciously taking His care for granted? Was I being careless about safety precautions and justifying it by calling it "trust"?

"He's unconscious!" they shouted.

The impact of their words finally hit me. I didn't wait to hear more. "He's in the van," I numbly heard as they followed me across the lawn.

"We're going to the hospital," Lloyd said in a calm, though unusually strained, voice.

"Bring my shoes and a wet towel," I called to the children as I climbed into the van.

By the time Lloyd had turned the van around, they had brought the things I had asked for.

"You all go and pray for Nathan," I said, shutting the door. The children looked forsaken and stricken as they watched us speed out the lane.

The speedometer maxed out as Lloyd guided the van along Elmridge Road to Route 11. We had a good half-hour drive ahead of us. Lloyd and I both started praying by turns or together, however it came out between the deep groanings of our spirits. As our prayers ended, Lloyd told me what had happened.

"Mary Ann," Lloyd began gently, "the back wheel of our big tractor rolled over Nathan's head. It will be a miracle if we can keep him."

I examined Nathan's head and face more closely. He seemed too fragile to move. His eyes were partly opened. I opened one, then the other. The right eye was rolled completely up in his head, and the left eye wasn't responding at all. *He's leaving us!* I thought. *Or his brain is not functioning . . .*

The blood wasn't gushing out of his ears anymore, but a slow trickle continued to reveal a serious fracture. A blood clot from his ear stuck to his shirt collar.

What a blessing this child had been to us these five years! Was God really going to take our Nathan home now? As I thought of the future without him, the days, months, and years ahead looked empty and cheerless. I remembered how we had committed Nathan to God when he was born. He was God's child and not our own. He was ours to care for only as long as God lent him to us. But no matter how surrendered I had thought my will, the parting looked very painful. Lloyd and I loved all our children, but now our strongest emotions were drawn to Nathan, who needed them most.

The miles seemed to drag in spite of the speeding van. *Will we ever get there?* I wondered. "O God, help us, help us now!" was the only prayer I could think of. I pressed Nathan's precious, unconscious, bleeding form gently to myself. I kissed him softly on his cool, dirty forehead. His irregular breathing was faltering, and momentarily it stopped. There was a gurgling sound in his throat. "He's not going to make it, Lloyd." I spoke quickly, calmly. The feeling of panic was gone. The calmness had to be from God. "I will be holding him in my arms when the death angel gently bears him away."

Tears came to my eyes—tears of grief, tears of parting, tears of love. The hardest of all were tears of remorse. Instinctively, I raised his head slightly. The gurgling sound, I discovered, was food. His stomach was rejecting its beef, mashed potatoes, and peas. The wet towels we had brought along came in very handy. Nathan resumed his irregular, gurgling, half-moaning breathing.

Lloyd and I had long had a theme song. We sang it on all special occasions. We sang it together when we were dating, on our wedding day, on anniversaries, and in any difficult or joyful experience. We sang it when each new baby was born, and now, after seventeen years of married life, we sang it again. We had just approached the red light at the Watertown city limits when Lloyd softly, falteringly started singing, "God moves in a mysterious way, His wonders to perform; He plants His footsteps in the sea and rides upon the storm."

*This must be a storm,* I pondered.

"Ye fearful saints, fresh courage take; the clouds ye so much dread are big with mercy and will break in blessings on your head."

*Even this?* I wondered. I bowed my head and meditated in reverence on the song's old yet ever-new message. I joined in the next verse but didn't get very far. "Judge not the Lord by feeble sense, but trust Him for His grace; behind a frowning providence He hides a smiling face."

*And we know that all things work together for good to them that love God, to them who are the called according to his purpose.* This familiar verse had become a faithful standby and echoed in our hearts just now.

Lloyd continued singing as I faltered. "His purposes will ripen fast, unfolding every hour; the bud may have a bitter taste, but sweet will be the flower."

*Is Nathan the bud? Will he soon bloom in Heaven?* I wondered.

"Blind unbelief is sure to err and scan His work in vain; God is His own interpreter, and He will make it plain."

*Yes, I want to trust Him, no matter what,* I resolved, blessed again by this song. The Lord had planned and managed our lives through joy and sorrow, and He would not stop now.

# 2.

# Suspense

*Underneath are the everlasting arms.*
*— Deuteronomy 33:27*

O ur oldest son Loyal could always be depended upon in a crisis. At age fifteen, he was a good manager, easily managing the herd records and charting under Lloyd's supervision. He was quick-witted and levelheaded.

Nathan's accident was no exception. It was Loyal who picked up Nathan's bloody form from the hard ground and held him on the tractor while Victor drove all the way to the barn. As soon as we started out the lane, Loyal called House of the Good Samaritan Hospital to inform them that we were on the way with an injured child. That's why a doctor wearing a white coat was standing outside awaiting our arrival.

It was a relief to drive up to the emergency room door. We had barely stopped before the van door was jerked open. "Is this the injured child?" the doctor said more than asked. He reached in and took Nathan from my arms and rushed through the sliding doors so fast we could hardly keep up. I had always taken care of the children when they were sick. I had nursed them through babyhood and helped them through teething, colic spells, and multiple illnesses. But this was beyond me, and I was grateful for the doctor.

The doctor laid Nathan on the emergency room table. Several professional workers began their responsibilities at once. The hospital's team was obviously well trained. Neurosurgeons, bone specialists, neurologists, an anesthesiologist, emergency room nurses, X-ray and lab technicians, and respiratory therapists each performed their jobs well. The most urgent need at the moment was blood. A child's veins are often small, especially when there is hardly any blood left in the child, so it was difficult to find veins for the IVs. The medical team worked silently and swiftly, making half-inch incisions in Nathan's skin at different places to access the veins. The necessary tubes were attached, and the skin was stitched together around the tubes. They called this a cutdown. They also checked Nathan for broken bones, ruptured spleen, lacerated liver, and other treatable conditions that could become life-threatening if left undiagnosed.

X-ray machines and other equipment were wheeled in. People came and went, but we were oblivious. Many hugged me and offered to pray for Nathan, but I could not remember later who they were. Lloyd and I answered questions automatically, hardly conscious of what was being asked.

Finally Lloyd said, "I'd better go out a while. I feel faint." I looked up at his white face and pale lips. He was escorted to a chair in the next room, but I stayed and watched a while longer. Soon I joined Lloyd on a lounge close by. Lloyd had called home. Allen and Carol, our pastor and his wife, were on their way to the hospital with clean clothes for me. Our other children rejoiced to know that their little brother was still alive, but their rejoicing was subdued by their concern.

A special meeting was called at church to pray for Nathan, committing him to God. This moved us to tears. We often felt blessed to be part of the spiritual brotherhood at Philadelphia Christian Fellowship Church. The eleven families in this more remote area of New York had gradually become part of our lives in the two years since our move from Pennsylvania. We hadn't chosen this area for any great financial possibilities. Other farming areas were more prosperous. But we liked the spirituality we saw in the brethren and the good environment a family farm would provide for our children.

I was in and out of the room to see what was happening and to find out how Nathan was doing. His right eye wasn't turned up in his head anymore and was responding. The left eye still showed no sign of response. "The wheel struck him here," someone was saying, pointing to the back of his head, which looked flatter and a bit out of shape. The tractor must have proceeded up the back of his head and down over his forehead. The bones of both ears were severely broken. Tread marks scarred his forehead. Several teeth were broken. The top of Nathan's head wasn't hurt and neither was his neck. It took us a long time to understand how an eighteen-inch-wide tractor tire could damage only a narrow space. Somehow, the wheel must not have put direct pressure on the top of his head. We thought of each child having a guardian angel and wondered if Nathan's angel hadn't, in mercy, lifted the tractor a little. It hardly seemed possible that his whole head hadn't been crushed.

"Hello! I'm Dr. Owen." A tall, light-complexioned, middle-aged man shook hands with both of us. "I'm a neurosurgeon and will be largely responsible for your son's care. I must inform you that his condition is very, very critical. His crushed skull is worse than a fracture. We will do what we can, but at this point we can only go minute by minute. Always with injuries like this there are blood clots on the brain. We will take a CT scan now. This is a sophisticated imaging device used to produce detailed X-ray pictures of the brain to help diagnose the problem," he explained. "The whole head is put inside the device and a picture is taken of the whole brain area. We will immediately proceed with surgery to remove any clots we find in these X-rays. He might not survive the operation, but serious brain damage will result if we don't remove the clots."

We signed the necessary papers and thanked him. Then we were ushered into a private waiting room on another floor. Every few minutes a nurse would come and share a detailed report of what was happening to Nathan. This kept us from imagining the worst. They answered all our questions patiently.

When Lloyd and I were finally alone to talk, weep, and pray, we spent some moments in earnest, heartfelt prayer. As we mingled our tears and poured out our grief to our heavenly Father, we drew from each other consolation and comfort. We knew our God was a God of love, but right then life seemed cruel. But not once did we lose faith in God's wisdom in knowing what was best. We continued to seek consolation from Him as we reviewed the whole afternoon in detail. Just how had the accident happened? Why had Nathan been riding on the tractor when we had decided the little ones should not ride on the tractor anymore?

Just two days before, when the boys had gone out to do the fieldwork, Nathan had run into the kitchen, crying. "Can I go along too, Mom? Just this once!" he begged. He had seen the other boys climb onto the tractor with his fourteen-year-old brother Victor.

Nathan's tears had fallen as I explained, "Justus and James are ten and eight years old. Father needs them to disc and harrow the field. You are only five. It's too dangerous for you. We don't want you to fall off the tractor and get hurt."

"I won't fall off, Mom." His large blue eyes had looked pleadingly into mine.

"Mama knows little boys love to ride on tractors, but not this time," I had insisted gently, but firmly, ignoring his disappointed tears. Lloyd and I were more interested in their obedience. We also shed tears sometimes when we were keenly disappointed. By submitting our will to God's will, we received sweet peace. Nathan meekly submitted when he saw that I wouldn't budge.

But today had been different. "We will be picking up rocks in the planted cornfield," Lloyd had announced to the family.

"Whose help would you like to have?" I asked.

"Many hands make light work," Lloyd replied good-naturedly. "Mother and the girls can stay in with Micah and Joshua. I'll take the rest of the boys with me."

I thought back to when I was a girl. We hadn't had many boys in our home, so we all went out to help pick up rocks in the fields. The youngest would guide the tractor through the field very slowly while the others threw rocks into the wagon or manure spreader.

Nathan hung back uncertainly after the other boys left the house. "Can I go along today, Mama?" he asked.

"Yes, since Father will be going along too. The cornfield is here by the barn, and the tractor goes very slowly for this kind of job."

He didn't wait to hear more, but darted out the door toward the barn.

"Boys, get started," Lloyd said. "I'll soon be there to help you. I want to finish fixing this pipe first."

So Nathan had gone along without Lloyd being aware of it. And I was not aware that Lloyd wasn't along, though even if he had been, he could not have prevented the accident. I also had not realized it wasn't the cornfield near the barn. Instead, it was the cornfield a mile back, and they had to drive over a bumpy field lane. The boys, knowing Nathan had permission, took him right along.

They reached the field, and the older boys jumped off to pick up rocks and turned the driving over to James. Nathan rode along on the tractor, holding on to the fender. James drove a few yards through the cornfield and then stopped to wait while the older boys threw stones into the wagon. The tractor jerked a bit as he started up again. Suddenly he heard a little sound like "oh" from Nathan. When he turned to see what was wrong, Nathan was gone.

# 3.
# Grief Shared

*Now no chastening for the*
*present seemeth to be joyous.*
*— Hebrews 12:11*

We hardly heard Dr. Minard walk into the room. He shook hands with us and immediately started talking. "We were all set up for the operation to remove the blood clots," he explained, "but the brain scan showed no clots. It's very unusual. We won't operate now, but will keep a minute-by-minute watch. He's in very critical condition. If Nathan makes it for twenty-four hours," he added, "he's got a chance. He is moving his left leg and groaning some."

No operation on our little boy's head. Not now, at least. It was like a mountain cast into the sea, and yet we knew bigger mountains loomed ahead of us.

"The nurses are hooking up a breathing machine now. He is breathing by himself, but if we do it this way, there will be less pressure on the brain. A tube will go into his mouth, down his esophagus, through his voice box, and into his lungs. It will breathe for him. And I want you to know, Mrs. Martin," he added softly and sympathetically, "my five-year-old rides on the tractor too."

Although they didn't dispel my feelings of remorse, his words were comforting.

Anna, a young sister from our church fellowship, stopped at the hospital on her way to work. It meant so much to share our grief with someone. Only a few minutes later, David and Carol, another of our pastors and his wife, appeared and stayed all evening. We were soon in one another's arms, weeping together. David and Carol had raised their family, and I often sought Carol's advice for child training or spiritual encouragement. Now I leaned on her for comfort as Lloyd and I poured out our aching hearts to them. Through the long evening they talked with us, wept with us, and shared our suffering in silence.

*I will not leave you comfortless. I will come to you.* The Lord engraved these words on our hearts. God was there "to revive the heart of the contrite ones" (Isaiah 57:15). The reality of death overwhelmed us. Though Nathan hadn't gone yet, we didn't entertain strong hopes that he would live, and yet moment by moment went by and he still lived. We so much expected death that we almost understood King David's relief when his child died. The relief from suspense gave him courage to arise and face life again.

Living in the warmth and peace of God doesn't shield us from pain. But the same God who created tears also provides the strength by faith to meet grief head-on. I had hurt deeply over incidents years ago. All had healed, and I hardly remembered them. I had thought nothing could really hurt me

anymore. I had felt strong and called it maturity. Only God
knows how to effectively break up fallow ground and help us
fully rely on Him and not be so self-sufficient.

But there was a feeling I couldn't shake; nor could I quite
face it. The little words "if only" sat like heavy rocks on our
broken hearts. We could claim the promise in Romans 8:28,
"We know that all things work together for good to them that
love God." But could we claim this verse for ourselves if our
own weakness had caused our innocent child to suffer?

*See God in everything* came to my mind. But this was something to work through. I had always been able to see God in
everything before, I thought. Financial difficulties had caused
us to trust Him more. I remembered those days. Illness had
taught us patience. Even death. My mother had died when I
was a small child. I still remembered the parting pain—my
confused mind trying to grasp death and understand the
adjustments that followed. Looking back, I know He was
in everything. Nearly every trial in life comes to us through
somebody's failure, ignorance, carelessness, or sin. If we can see
God's hand in it, the experience has a sweetness that consoles
while it wounds.

I voiced my guilt aloud, and David answered, "We can't
condemn ourselves for what happened. Think of God having
multiple purposes for one incident." His encouragement was
the beginning of working through my guilty feelings. Jesus
came to wash our sins away and forgive us.

"You may see your son now," a kind nurse was saying. "He's
all set up in the intensive care unit. You may come whenever
you want and stay as long as you like. You may use this lounge

here to rest, or we will gladly pull a recliner into the room beside his bed."

The four of us followed her into the room. White gauze enveloped Nathan's head. Tubes were connected all over him with monitors attached. Blood was flowing into his veins through IV tubes. We put our arms around him and tenderly kissed him, but there was no response.

"It's good to talk to him," the nurse assured us. "Subconsciously he knows you're there and feels the comfort and reassurance of being with someone he knows."

We stood silently at his bedside and took in the almost lifeless form of our lively little boy. He was a sensitive and expressive child who had known very little pain or sickness. At three years old he had liked to tell others the Bible stories he knew. Jonah and the whale was his favorite. But he tended to be a daring child. I had never thought of telling a four-year-old that he was too young to climb a fifty-foot silo. I'd never imagined he'd try it, because our older boys were afraid to climb it. But sure enough, one day he climbed clear to the top of the empty silo, looked out over the countryside, and then climbed back down again.

I grew weak all over when I heard about it. "Nathan, what if you had fallen?" I asked him sternly.

"I held on really tight, Mom," he responded, his serious blue eyes looking into mine. He was strictly warned not to do it again until he was older.

Another time I had looked out the kitchen window to see my four-year-old boy sitting on top of the horizontal elevator outside the barn. Holding on to the bars at the top of the elevator, he again was looking out over the countryside. I hardly knew whether I ought to call him or not. What if I scared him and he lost his grip and dropped to the ground thirty feet below? I sighed in relief as he climbed down slowly.

Nathan loved schoolwork even though he didn't go to school yet. Coloring, cutting, books, letters, and writing were his delight. He had been eager to start school in the fall. But now I couldn't even imagine the unknown, complicated future. Just the day before I had told some of the children at the dinner table, "In this life sometimes we suffer and are not comfortable, but it is only for a short time. Eternity is forever." Did I really believe that? Could I live it for them?

David and Lloyd laid their hands on Nathan's bruised, broken little head and prayed for his recovery. "And Father," David begged as he brought his prayer to a close, "may this be an experience that astonishes even the doctors and nurses so they will marvel at Your miraculous healing power."

The doctors kept a close watch on Nathan. "We will take another CT scan to show the extent of his brain damage and tell you the results," Dr. Owen explained.

David and Carol went home, leaving Lloyd and me alone with Nathan. We stood silently beside his bed. I didn't have the courage to insist that God make him well. I knew that He could, but somehow I sensed the difficult, painful, and perhaps incomplete road to recovery ahead, and I felt unwilling to face it. We sought God's will. Lloyd opened his Bible. A verse in Job 38 stood out vividly. "Have the gates of death been opened unto thee?" The gates of death were open wide to Nathan, and we were seeing into its shadow.

We honestly wanted to bow our wills to God's will. We thought of incidents we knew of children who had almost died. God had granted life and health, but they had grown up to fill sinners' graves. "So, Father," we prayed by Nathan's bedside, holding his little hands in ours, "if You in your foreknowledge know this will happen to our child, please take him right now. May all prayers for his recovery be unheeded. And please, God," we wept from our aching hearts, "give us the grace for this parting."

As our souls were bowed before God, we willingly committed our darling son to death and the grave. A new hope seemed to be born in our hearts—courage from the Resurrected One whose death on the cross meant life for us.

The next boost of courage came from a Catholic boy we would learn to know very well in the next few weeks. His words helped fan that spark of hope. Andy was a young, enthusiastic, gentlemanly person. He seemed more mature than the average nineteen-year-old. He approached us as old friends and immediately came to the point.

"I'm sorry about what happened to your son," he began. "But I want to tell you that you've got a tremendous doctor. There isn't another doctor like him in the state of New York. Our Mary Beth," he continued, "flew out of the back of a pickup truck on an inflated rubber raft. She landed headfirst on a cement culvert and has been in a coma for three weeks. She's had three operations, and twice she developed spinal meningitis from infection, but she is now responding and communicating with us. She squeezes our hands and her eyes are partly open. There really is hope for your son's recovery if there is hope for Mary Beth.

"And don't feel guilty about what happened," he added. "I was driving the truck when we went over the bump that bounced her out. I had to seek forgiveness and forgive myself and go on with life."

At ten o'clock, Lloyd reluctantly went home. I couldn't consider leaving Nathan, but someone needed to be home with our other children. Allen and Sadie, friends from church, had stayed with our children through the long afternoon. Allen had helped the boys fix a water bowl in the barn and befriended them through the suspenseful evening. And Sadie's quiet ways had perfectly suited the children's mood.

During that long afternoon, Allen overheard one of the boys asking James, "Why didn't you stop the tractor when you saw Nathan fall?"

James answered abruptly, "I would have stopped right on his head!"

Later, James sat on the couch staring into space, unconscious of his surroundings. At eight years old he was pretty young to carry the guilt of driving over his little brother. Allen sat down by his side and took his hand. "James," he said softly, kindly drawing him back to reality, "it wasn't your fault that Nathan fell off the tractor. You couldn't have done anything about it. You were driving slowly and doing what you were supposed to do. We are praying for Nathan, and God will take care of him."

A smile of relief slowly spread over James's face as his huge brown eyes looked up trustingly to Allen.

"Would you show me the calves in the barn?" Allen asked. "I'd like to see them."

Phone calls poured in from neighbors, friends, and relatives. Most offered to pray for Nathan and for us. But one couple from our church told us, "We are going to pray for healing for the boy who was driving the tractor." We were grateful. Feelings of guilt, even when they are undeserved, can leave scars that remain years later.

God in His mercy was afflicting our family to draw us closer to Him and to help us learn important lessons. He was also comforting us according to our individual needs through whatever avenues He chose—through His Word, His church, verses, letters, cards, phone calls, and many other ways.

Another couple gave us a card the day after the accident. We drank deeply of the inspiring verses they had chosen. "Blessed be . . . the God of all comfort; who comforteth us in all our tribulation" (2 Corinthians 1:3, 4). "Commit thy way unto the LORD; trust also in him; and he shall bring it to pass" (Psalm 37:5). "He healeth the broken in heart, and bindeth up their wounds" (Psalm 147:3). "He which hath begun a good work in you will perform it" (Philippians 1:6). "For my thoughts are not your thoughts, neither are your ways my ways, saith the LORD" (Isaiah 55:8).

# 4.

# A Time of Suffering

*O satisfy us early with thy mercy;*
*that we may rejoice and be glad all our days.*
*— Psalm 90:14*

God never changes. His heart motive remains the same through time and eternity. His desire is to show love and forgiveness to us. If we are hurt, sick, or going through difficulties, our Father in Heaven seems closer to us. Sometimes our flesh is repulsive to Him because of sin, but He wants to clean us and continue to love us. It's just like when our children go out to play and get all muddy or dirty. We bring them in and wash them. The mud is rejected, but we accept the child.

My mind churned through many of these thoughts as I lay on the cot in the lounge, trying to get some rest during the long night. As God's heart reached out to us, our hearts reached out to our son. Every hour or so I went to Nathan's bedside, stooped over his unconscious form, and talked to him even though he didn't respond. Then I went back to my cot and tried to rest again. It was a night of suffering and prayer, of seeking God's will, weeping alone, and sorting out my thoughts and deepest emotions before God. I turned to the Word of God. Verses in Psalms about mercy stood out in a special way. No matter how rough the experience, a heart that is open can see God's mercy. I drew from and found comfort in the Psalms. "The Lord is merciful and gracious, slow to anger, and plenteous in mercy. He will not always chide: neither will he keep his anger forever. He hath not dealt with us after our sins; nor rewarded us according to our iniquities" (Psalm 103:8-10). "For in the time of trouble he shall hide me in his pavilion: in the secret of his tabernacle shall he hide me; he shall set me up upon a rock" (Psalm 27:5). A rock is a symbol of security to a tempest-tossed soul. It's solid and won't move. It's always there. This rock is Jesus, who never fails us.

A few times during the night I grew sleepy and settled down to rest. As I would begin to doze off, I would see Nathan's little head under a tractor wheel. I would awaken with a jolt only to have the painful truth stab repeatedly at my already wounded heart.

Yes, it was a night of suffering. For the rest of the early hours of the morning I stayed by Nathan's bedside.

Lloyd got a little sleep at home and was at the hospital early the next morning. He had also been reading Psalms, and even some of the same verses. The verses that impressed Lloyd most were, "God be merciful unto us, and bless us; and cause his face to shine upon us; that thy way may be known upon earth, thy saving health among all nations" (Psalm 67:1, 2). (People in other nations were hearing about Nathan's accident through Lloyd's brothers in Paraguay and British Columbia.)

\* \* \*

"Jesus loves me this I know, for the Bible tells me so. Little ones to Him belong. They are weak but He is strong." We sang other songs by Nathan's bedside, but we sang this one the most. Later the head nurse told me she had a meeting with the ladies at her church. They all sang "Jesus Loves Me" in honor of Nathan. A lot of people we met at the hospital were touched by Nathan's experience, and we were touched because so many people seemed to truly care. Many put their arms around me and promised to pray for him. Some said their church groups or prayer circles were praying for Nathan and us. We also spent hours with close relatives of others who were suffering. Listening and sharing their burdens helped to lighten ours.

It was hard to hold Nathan's hand because it was strapped down to protect the IVs and other tubes in his arm. He couldn't make a sound because of the air tube through his voice box. Blood still trickled from his ears. Later it turned to a clear liquid and also flowed from his nose and mouth. The nurses faithfully kept prying his eyes open and shining a flashlight into them. His right eye was responding, but his left one wasn't. This indicated something wrong in the brain. He knew when the nurses were working on him. The only part of his body he could move was his left leg. This he kicked viciously until they gave him Valium to keep him calm. His expression looked like he was crying. He calmed when I put my arm around him and sang, talked, or prayed. The nurses were right—he did know familiar voices subconsciously. The nurses assured me that familiar voices also draw patients back to reality sooner.

"This tiny tube," Mrs. Marge, the head nurse, explained to Lloyd and me, "is to monitor the pressure in the skull. If the pressure goes up to twenty, there is danger of severe brain damage. If that happens we will drill a tiny hole in the skull. You see," she explained, "when a brain is injured, it swells, just like any other part of the body. The pressure causes brain damage. In three days the swelling reaches its peak; then it begins to subside."

"What will we do if it goes that high?" we asked. We were learning fast to ask questions. We desperately wanted to understand everything that was going on.

"We are watching it closely," she continued. "If it goes up to eighteen, we give medication. So far that has brought it down. But if it doesn't, we will operate to relieve the pressure. The next three days will be crucial."

We helped watch the monitor's needle. A few times we saw it go dangerously high. Those times found us interceding to the God of all comfort, asking for His mercy. Prayer! That was the work we could do to help Nathan. We entered into it with purpose and continued until we felt assured of the results. We knew we had to be completely surrendered to God's will. So with broken, surrendered wills, we plunged into His presence as though a life depended on it. A life *did* depend on God. The small, isolated lounge room down the hall became a private prayer closet for us where we fought many a battle to conquer our wills and emotions.

The brethren and sisters from our church came one by one. Most of them tenderly laid hands on our little darling's bruised, broken head and prayed, graciously lifting him to the tender heart of our Father. Samuel and his wife Miriam were regular visitors. As a former city policeman, he was well acquainted with accidents and the sufferings of mankind. Their tender hearts moved them to tears, to prayer, and to visit us almost daily.

Lloyd had a long, serious conversation with our new friend Andy, who drank in truth from the Scriptures. It helped us to know that maybe through Nathan's injury some soul would come closer to the truth of salvation through faith and the blessedness of traveling the straight and narrow way.

I went home the second night while Lloyd stayed at the hospital, but again I did not sleep. But there is satisfaction in a night awake with God. I knew others had had children snatched from their homes—sometimes by death—but I'd also heard stories from Communist countries where children were taken to children's homes and indoctrinated in atheism. It helped put our experience in perspective to think of those who had survived worse experiences.

Nathan continued to kick ferociously even though he was in a coma. His suffering was evident, and this pained our hearts. The shocking vision of Nathan's little head under a tractor wheel still haunted me whenever I dozed off. The Lord specifically impressed on our minds the short but profound verse, "Continue in prayer" (Colossians 4:2). We were weary in body, but were resting in God's comfort and healing power both for ourselves and our severely injured son.

"Our precious little Nathan!" Our oldest daughter's tender heart bled as she expressed her feelings. "It just hurts," Keturah continued in tears. We shared and tried to comfort one another with as bright an outlook as we could. Of all our children, Keturah would miss Nathan most, since she, at sixteen, was like a second mother to the little boys. When the older children were at school, Nathan trailed her, asking, "Keturah, how do you do this? What can I do next?" She usually had some creative suggestion to occupy his young mind. She made pictures to color and objects to match. He loved these projects, and they helped prepare him for school. If I had to leave for the day, Keturah was quite capable of going on with the housework. The little boys loved her stories, her attention, and her affection.

"Is Nathan going to die?" Hannah too felt Nathan's absence deeply. She was a real leader and playmate for our younger boys. They loved her bike rides, made-up games, and cheerful ways. If she wasn't around on a Sunday afternoon, they seemed forlorn and didn't know what to do. We needed her very much around the house, since we had only two girls. With seven brothers, it was no wonder her interest fluctuated between housework and outdoor things.

Our children's faith often inspired us. Without knowing just how they would be provided for, they trusted that it would be done. We, who have a heavenly Father watching over us, can trust Him in the same way that children trust the adults around them. Even in our pain, He allows us to feel the continued prayers and love of friends, which are an ointment that soothes the ache.

# 5.

# Fluctuating Hopes

*The cup which my Father hath given me,*
*shall I not drink it?*
*— John 18:11*

The long corridors, elevators, sliding doors, and the sterilized white atmosphere of the hospital were fast becoming home to us. The hospital routine and personnel, even the smells, were imprinting our lives. We felt torn between our loyalty to our children at home and Nathan. But Nathan needed us most. In our quiet moments alone, we pondered God's purpose for this experience. But we didn't have to know why. Our job was to submit and reap the benefit.

As I sat by Nathan's bed, I recalled a scene from just a few days before. The sunset was mellowing its magnificent gold-orange and purple rays in emerald brightness as I drove the Datsun slowly out the bumpy farm lane. The boys, busy planting corn in our back fields, always appreciated a cool drink when they were working. There were not many quiet moments during the day with nine healthy, active children in the family, so this was a rare moment when I was alone. As a youth, I had always loved to take my Bible and a songbook and go for a walk to be alone with God. Something about the fields and the wide open spaces always drew my soul toward Him.

On this day, a very real burden weighed on my heart as I drove the two-mile stretch. I didn't know what it was. I cried to the Lord from the depth of my soul, not for anything in particular, but for the needs of mankind in general. I prayed for myself and some of my careless ways; for my dear husband, who worked so hard to support us all; and for each of the children individually, according to their personal needs. I interceded for the church and the local community, that God would touch hearts and motivate souls to seek Him. Somehow, I keenly felt the need of God's presence in our lives and in our home.

Now, as I remembered that prayer, my thoughts drifted to the evening before, when Curvin and Kathy had come to visit us in the hospital. We had sat in the lounge as they blended their soft voices melodiously in a few songs. One song had expressed the deep inner desire and burden of my heart.

> Oh, give us homes built firm upon the Saviour,
> Where Christ is head and counselor and guide;
> Where every child is taught His love and favor
> And gives his heart to Christ, the crucified.
> How sweet to know that though his footsteps waver
> His faithful Lord is working by His side![1]

---

1. The words and music to this song are at the end of this book.

The wonderful thing about building a Christian home is that we don't need a wonderful location with fine landscaping and panoramic views. It doesn't have to have the latest appliances or the best furniture. It can be elaborately furnished with the priceless virtues of love, joy, peace, and kindness. And its foundation is Jesus Christ. He planned and started the first home and is more than willing to help us build ours.

*Are you willing to go through whatever it takes?* The thought came to me vividly, forcefully. *Whatever it takes,* I thought. Those were scary words. This was the God who put Jonah in the whale's belly. He could give life and take life. I shrank from suffering. But I knew my merciful Father cared and would not let anything happen more than I could bear. So I confessed through my tears, "Yes, Lord, whatever it takes."

The burden lifted from my heart. All was in God's hands. My life and my loved ones. He would refine us and manage our growth and maturity in Him.

I stood beside Nathan's bed and looked down at his broken head, comforted by faith, and whispered, "I believe our Father in Heaven has a loving heart. Though He allows grief, yet He will have compassion according to the multitudes of His mercies. For He does not afflict us without purpose."

I hardly felt like calling friends. It just seemed easier to evade people, even kind ones. But others cared, called, and came. Friends and relatives called from other states. Neighbors and friends from church offered whatever help we needed. Those who came comforted us by being good listeners as much as by what they said.

My older sister Karen and I had been especially close as children, but hundreds of miles separated us now. We four younger children, all close in age, had turned to each other for support when our mother was taken from our home into the glories of Heaven. We were placed in other homes for a while and then reunited to face the adjustments of another mother, another community, another school, another church, and another culture. We clung together through these adjustments because we were a part of each other's secure world. Now who would drive 370 miles to come see us but my sister Karen and her husband and their family. It was always difficult to convince Grandpa to travel, but he readily came along with Karen to see Nathan. Their weekend stay was a boost to all of us. Ellen, Karen's oldest daughter, stayed at the house to help our girls with the work. Karen and Grandpa stayed with me all morning at the hospital while the rest of the family went to church. Grandpa related Psalm 79:11 to unconscious Nathan: "Let the sighing of the prisoner come before thee; according to the greatness of thy power preserve thou those that are appointed to die."

Lloyd shared with the church the verses from Psalms that had so comforted us during the first long night. They brought tears to nearly everyone's eyes.

Lloyd and I were developing a workable schedule with day and night shifts. He preferred the night shift with Nathan. He needed to be home with the boys in the daytime to help with and supervise the work. There was more going on with Nathan during the day, so I preferred the day shift. The children eagerly waited for my arrival at home at seven or eight o'clock.

They came from all directions with lots of questions. I tried to explain Nathan's progress. It seemed to be an emotional release for them to talk and talk. It was always late before I retired at night. But I took time to be alone with God no matter how late it was. The Lord was with us, and in our distress He spoke comfort directly to our needs and gave us strength to go on.

Monday, Nathan was still in a coma. Just three days before, we had been given no reason to hope that he would still be alive. Yet he was. His eyes were closed and he gave no response when we talked to him, but the nurses insisted he could hear us and was comforted by us. So we sang and talked to him. We learned that there are different stages and depths of unconsciousness. The nurses explained the things they did to test for responses. "Nathan twitches when he is pinched on his right foot. That means he has a little feeling in his right side even though that side is paralyzed," one explained. "It may seem cruel to pinch him, but it helps us to know if there is progress. The next step is movement. It may be aimless and uncoordinated, but we watch for that. What we really want is movement on command, which means that his brain can effectively relay the command to his extremities. Nathan jerks whenever he is pinched, so he has feeling, and more could come back."

Our hopes rose with these reports, and we praised God for every movement and response.

Allen and Sadie visited faithfully. Allen spoke to Nathan like an old friend. Something about Nathan's expression convinced us that he knew when we were there.

We were often impressed with the skill of the medical professionals. We were satisfied that we had the best doctor available. A phrase in Hebrews 1:3 caught my attention, and I pondered it for a long time: "upholding all things by the word of his power." I shared it with Lloyd, and we were encouraged to put our complete trust in God for Nathan's recovery and not to trust in the doctors, no matter how skilled. We were reminded that things don't just happen according to natural sequences, but all things are in God's control. By His spoken word the world was created. Gravity, the weather, and even ruling powers were created, established, and controlled by God. It revived our spirits tremendously to rest in the fact that all the complications surrounding Nathan's recovery were small matters to God, for whom all things are possible. This inspiration helped prepare us for the next difficult experience.

# 6.
# Other Mountains Removed

*Consider him ... lest ye be wearied*
*and faint in your minds.*
*— Hebrews 12:3*

God does not dispense strength and encouragement like a
druggist fills a prescription. The Lord doesn't give us pills
to take so we can handle our weary moments. He promises
Himself. That is all. That is more than enough! In our pain and
exhaustion and spiritual fatigue, He will give us rest, "For he is
our peace" (Ephesians 2:14).

I had known weary moments before. Like the time when the
children had whooping cough. Hannah was only five months
old and had a severe case. Sometimes I sat in the rocking chair
almost all night holding her. With each coughing spell I felt I
had to help her catch her breath again. I had heard of babies
dying from this disease. The other children were two, three, and

four years old. They also had severe cases that brought me to their rooms with almost every coughing spell. The days stretched into weeks, and I lost so much sleep that I couldn't sleep even when I had the chance. At the point of sheer exhaustion, when my tears were all shed and my strength gone, I started to thank the Lord. I knew this experience was for a purpose. He was in control. After that I could sit in my rocking chair and overflow with praise and thanksgiving to my Lord. I experienced 2 Corinthians 12:9 in a very real way: "For my strength is made perfect in weakness. Most gladly therefore will I rather glory in my infirmities, that the power of Christ may rest upon me."

We began to recognize this same strength through our long days and nights with Nathan. Truly our God was supplying all our needs according to His riches in glory by Christ Jesus (Philippians 4:19).

Three days Jonah was in the whale's belly. Oh, the delight he must have felt to be suddenly thrown into sunshine and freedom on solid land! Three days Jesus tasted of death. Mary Magdalene and the other Mary grieved when they sought to show their last respect to Jesus' dead body but couldn't find it. Then they heard the triumphant words, "He is risen!"

Lloyd and I felt in a small way how those women must have felt. For three days we looked at Nathan's crooked, swollen face. His draining ears, nose, and mouth were a constant reminder of what appeared to be a hopeless injury.

But Tuesday morning we were thrilled! (And that's putting it mildly.)

I may have seemed a little uncontrolled when I called the nurses to come and look at Nathan. I had been bending over his precious form, my arm around his waist, talking to him about the new calf, the haymow—anything familiar. I shared almost everything that came to my mind with him. All at once his right eye opened slowly and his blue eye looked directly into mine. The nurses hurried over and shared my excitement. They talked to him, wrote notes to other nurses, and exclaimed over the sign of progress.

"Over here's Mama," I said gently. He responded to my voice and very noticeably turned his eye toward me. His left eye was swollen shut so tightly that he couldn't have opened it if he had tried. Both eyes were beginning to respond properly with the routine flashlight procedure. But we knew there was more to seeing than simply having the eyes open. It takes a mind to understand what the eyes see.

Tuesday afternoon Dr. Owen, Nathan's neurosurgeon, came to Nathan's bedside to talk to Lloyd and me. He pulled up a chair and sat down facing us. Then he honestly and sincerely told us the painful truth. "I'm sorry to tell you," he began, "but the last CT scan revealed a damaged area on the left side of Nathan's brain, similar to that left by a stroke. This dark area was three or four inches in diameter." He paused as he saw the puzzled, shocked expressions on our faces. "This has paralyzed the right side of his body. You see, the left side of the brain controls the right side of the body. We can't tell yet how permanent the damage is, but it will affect his speech and learning."

He proceeded to explain more about the workings of the brain, but I didn't hear any more for a while. Speech and learning! Slowly but surely the words sank in. I felt the monster of uncertainty and fear attacking my newfound faith and courage.

"We will certainly do what we can," I heard Dr. Owen saying, "and we will go on from day to day." He had said minute by minute that first day, then hour by hour. Now he was saying day by day. "Don't expect too much," he added before walking out. "He may be here two to four months. Then rehabilitation hospitals offer further therapy for damaged minds."

Neither Lloyd nor I spoke for a few minutes after Dr. Owen left the room. We stood, speechless, gazing upon the form of our once active son. Our hopes had slowly risen over the past few days for Nathan's complete recovery. But now our hopes were dashed. Nathan would never walk, never talk, never learn, never go to school like other children. He was paralyzed and crippled for life.

"But God . . ." Lloyd spoke first as we stared at Nathan's unconscious form. Those two little words made a tremendous difference. "God is our refuge and strength, a very present help in trouble," Lloyd quoted Psalm 46:1. "Two and a half thousand years ago they sang that. It is for us today." Lloyd was trying to console himself as much as me. "We must remember that the doctor told us this because he felt it was his duty. We appreciate him, but doesn't God have any say in this?"

Suddenly I remembered the phrase "upholding all things by the word of his power." Our souls were sick and weary, and we crept under the wings of our loving Saviour. We sank down in anguish to pour out our hearts without uttering a word. There we began to experience what Jesus promised His friends: "My peace I give unto you: not as the world giveth" (John 14:27). Later, alone in the washroom, I was led directly to a verse as I opened my Bible. God knew the hopeless feelings in my heart, and I didn't even have to search. The words in Psalm 41 left their impression on me as I drank them in. "The LORD will preserve him, and keep him alive; and he shall be blessed upon the earth. The LORD will strengthen him upon the bed of languishing: thou wilt make all his bed in his sickness." I read and reread the passage; then I shared it with Lloyd. He, in turn, shared the words he was meditating on. He was led to 1 Kings 17 while leafing though his worn Bible. The widow's son died, and there was no hope of enjoying his presence again. But the widow's son was restored to life. Lloyd could identify with the woman's distress. He read over the passage, letting the miracle of divine healing refresh his spirit. We found ourselves having faith in receiving a miracle for our son, though we hardly had the faith to ask. We sang, "Elijah's God still lives today, O blessed be His name. And when His children to Him pray, He answers still the same." In the Epistle of James, Lloyd read how Elijah was a man subject to the same weaknesses we are. He prayed. God honored his prayer and granted his request. Then Lloyd read again about the widow's son being raised to life, and it seemed like God had a similar experience in view for our son.

We wanted to be willing to accept whatever God had for us, but we felt more and more inspired to pray for restoration of Nathan's health. We were again receiving thoughts of courage, faith, and restoration from the Bible. I clutched at these thoughts and verses like a drowning person grasping for something solid.

Tuesday night they took the monitor off Nathan's brain. The pressure had stayed down, which meant that the brain swelling was going down. Another prayer had been answered and another surgery averted. God had moved another mountain in the path of Nathan's healing. But there were more mountains on the long road to recovery.

The doctors and nurses were always willing to take time to patiently explain anything we wanted to know. We asked a lot of questions. Even though Nathan had escaped two operations, we soon understood that he faced the possibility of another one.

The doctor's gravest concern now was the profuse leakage of cerebrospinal fluid from Nathan's ears, nose, and mouth. The brain and spinal cord are bathed in this fluid, which is contained in a lining around these structures. If the membranes forming this lining or sac around the brain get punctured or torn, bacteria can get in and cause infection. Nathan was kept on a special intravenous antibiotic to prevent this.

"We may have to operate to stop this leakage," Dr. Owen said. "We cut under the upper lip, go through the nasal cavity into the brain, and seal off the leakages we can find. Sometimes it takes more than one operation. The operation increases the risk of meningitis, but we have been very successful in preventing and treating this."

Again, we asked for prayer. Many trusted prayer warriors were praying on Nathan's behalf.

The miraculous answers to prayer so far had greatly strengthened our faith. Nevertheless, each new incident we faced put us through another struggle. We had to learn to trust God and not be fearful. We knew all was in His control, but we faced deep hurts and dark hours. God didn't give us the grace to overcome a week in advance. He gave us the grace to bring us through one day at a time. This kept us coming back for more. And God's perfect timing brought mail and encouragement from others just when we needed it most.

Sometimes we think of the year's close as marking the end of a chapter in our lives. Now it seemed like each day was a new chapter. We drew from the Book of Job in the Bible. Nothing could have prepared him for all the bad news he heard that day. Imagine his feelings when he heard, "You've lost your livestock; they've all been stolen. Your sheep and camels were destroyed. Your servants were murdered. Oh, and one more thing. Your children were crushed when the house fell during a windstorm. All ten are dead." Job got all this news in a five-minute period. Just when Job needed his wife's support most, she gave in to her own despair and uttered those hopeless words, "Curse God and die!" His enduring answer is remarkable: "Shall we accept good from God and not adversity?" His faith sustained him through the turbulence he faced later from his physical suffering and his miserable comforters. Lloyd and I were encouraged by Romans 11:33, "O the depth of the riches both of the wisdom and knowledge of God! How unsearchable are his judgments, and his ways past finding out!"

A dye test located the leakage, and the operation was scheduled. The saints were praying. The morning of the operation we were amazed and delighted to be firsthand witnesses of another act of God. The fluid stopped draining completely. God had sealed off those injured areas, and no operation was necessary after all. A few doctors examined Nathan and remarked, "It must be your prayers, Mrs. Martin. It must be God." We had begun to hear such remarks regularly from the medical people, and we responded by giving all the glory to God. We continued to thank and praise Him.

Others were also looking on and drawing strength from our experience. Samuel told us later, "As I face trials, tests, and discouragements in life, I need a real act of God to strengthen my faith. All I need to do is look at Nathan and see what God is doing for him. Then I receive the shot of courage I need."

Cousin Ellen and Keturah went to the hospital on the sixth morning instead of me. I stayed home and had breakfast with Lloyd and the rest of the family. It was so nice to be together. Everyone wanted to talk at once. Joshua, our one-year-old, had stopped crying every time I came and went. Children adjust to adverse situations quickly, but it gripped my heart every time I had to leave. We tried to explain to Micah why we had to leave so often. He was only three years old, and the rejection he was feeling came out in naughtiness. We put forth greater effort to show our love for him and give him more attention.

When Nathan seemed to be in almost constant pain, we became very specific and desperate in our prayers. It seemed urgent to persevere in prayer. We needed to constantly abide in the secret place of the Most High, enjoying His blessing and closeness, committing everything to Christ. It made us feel secure in God as we read the verse, "Many prophets have desired to know the things that you know and have not known them." We thanked God for the valuable things we were learning from this school of suffering and prayed we would always remember.

# 7.

# Through More Shadows

*I will fear no evil: for thou art with me.*
*— Psalm 23:4*

Mrs. Sanders, one of the intensive care unit nurses, shared her tragic experience with us. When she was a girl, the barn caught fire one night. They never knew what started it, but her father ran into the barn to try to free some cattle. He never reappeared. Her father was burned with the barn, cattle, and implements. His heart may have failed or he may have been overcome by the smoke. They will never know for sure. But they knew the anguish and the healing that followed.

Hearing about tragedies in the lives of others helped us endure our own. Mrs. Sanders had known that it would.

On our shift change, Lloyd and I always shared with one another the verses or promises God had given us that day.

Lloyd drew from James 5 about enduring, and I always found strength in my favorite chapter, Luke 18. I don't think there is any Scripture I turned to as often as the story of this woman who persevered in spite of the fact that her requests could be rejected by an unjust judge. The secret was that she didn't give up believing. I received a letter at this time that blended in beautifully with this Scripture and greatly strengthened my faith. "We're praying that your little boy will be all right again. Several people in the Bible said to Jesus, 'I know You can if You will. Lord, increase our faith.' We pray that it might be the Lord's will to restore him whole."

God tests and honors our faith and then rewards us speedily. It may not seem speedy to us, but God works behind the scenes in ways we are not aware of. God tests our attitudes toward Him. If we let ourselves go to pieces, we can't develop the maturity and strength God wants us to develop. It helped to hear stories of what others had gone through. Hearing about the barn fire made me remember a frightening experience that had strengthened our faith years ago. We had been lingering at the dinner table. Our two children, ages one and two, were napping upstairs. I was spring housecleaning and burning a lot of trash in the open fireplace of an old washhouse attached to our house. Suddenly through the kitchen window we noticed the fire was out of hand. Intense black smoke filled the washhouse, and the flames leapt higher than the fireplace. Lloyd dashed for the fire, and I lost no time going for the children. We both knew that if the washhouse burned, the whole house would burn. The startled children were safely transported to the lawn. But when I looked for Lloyd, all I could see was the hose on the outside spigot leading into the smoky building. I screamed his name. No answer. In my panic I didn't even think of calling the firehouse. All I could imagine was my husband overcome with smoke in a burning building. A prayer burst forth from my heart. An interminable minute or two later, Lloyd dashed from the doorway of the smoky building. He hadn't heard me call because he had knocked out the glass and stuck his head out the window on the other side of the washroom so he could breathe. Then he had ducked back in and sprayed water furiously on the fire until it was out. We both praised God and thanked Him for His protection.

Remembering these answered prayers of the past helped us to pray in faith now.

The pastor on call at the hospital stopped by each day and spoke words of encouragement. I never tired of sharing with anyone who showed an interest in Nathan's progress. But it was special when the brothers and sisters from our church came in. We felt a special bond with those we regularly worshiped with.

Nathan continued to watch us silently. His one open eye followed our every move during his waking hours. Occasionally we had to leave the room for necessities of our own or because they were doing some medical procedure. His face would pucker up and cry, but no voice or tears came because of the breathing-machine tube through his windpipe. He couldn't utter a sound. When we came back into his room, he was very glad to see us. The nurses soon let us stay for more and more of the medical procedures.

We still had so many questions. We were certain Nathan knew us. But did he remember anything? Was he bewildered?

Did he know where he was? We often put our arms around him and explained, "Nathan, you are in the hospital. You were hurt. You fell off the tractor." We did not tell him for a long time that the tractor actually ran over his head. We didn't know how he would handle that. "These ladies are nurses. They are very nice. They love you too." At first we didn't know if he was getting the message, but later we were sure he understood. He relaxed better and cooperated more with the nurses once he knew they were trying to help him and not torment him.

We wondered how permanent the damage was to his brain, but there was no way to know. We just had to wait and see. Waiting is often more difficult than doing something to help. Psalm 37:7 tells us how to wait: "Rest in the LORD, and wait patiently for him." With patience we can rest in the Lord while we wait. I was not a patient person by nature. I would get upset when I was ready to go someplace and had to wait on someone. But I had spent lots of time in God's waiting room. God had to take me through difficult experiences in life to teach me patience.

Nathan's bed had gathered quite a collection of teddy bears and little animals in the week he had been in the hospital. Stanley, a Christian youth from our church, had always showed an interest in the little boys and their world. Nathan considered this young man one of his best friends. He always looked forward to going to church and talking with Stan, as he liked to call him. Now Stan had sent Nathan a teddy bear dressed like a farmer with a crooked straw hat and bib overalls. Others, too, had sent stuffed animals. To pass the time and to entertain Nathan, I started playing with his teddies where he could watch me. We acted out stories and the teddies sat on Nathan. They jumped all over the bed, talking to one another. He could not move his head, but he watched with his one open eye as much as he could.

I grew weary of entertaining that way too, wondering what to do or say next to entertain a five-year-old I wasn't even sure knew what I was doing. Finally I said, "Nathan, if you want me to stop playing with your animals, squeeze your eye shut." He just kept staring at me. My heart sank at my conclusion: He doesn't even understand that much. But I tried again. "Nathan, if you want me to keep playing with the teddies, squeeze your eye shut like this." And I showed him by squeezing my right eye tightly shut. I jumped when he responded to my request by squeezing his eye tightly shut. He wanted me to keep playing! What was more, he understood! And was able to respond!

The nurses shared my excitement. "You are stimulating his mind," they praised. "This will help him come back to reality sooner. The stimulation encourages brain activity."

With this knowledge and encouragement, together with the burst of excitement, I went a little overboard in my attempts at therapy. I plunged into stimulating him like his life depended on it. Lloyd joined in, and the visitors who came helped too. It became a real game. We asked a lot of questions: "Does your head hurt? Does your belly hurt? Which nurse do you like best? Who do you remember?" He answered by shutting his eye according to which answer was right. Sometimes I noticed that he was mixed up and gave a wrong answer. When his mind grew tired, we stopped for a while. But we were actively involved in the real world of our son's mind, which had been locked from us for about a week. Later he grew weary of shutting his eye and started to nod his head to answer questions. We were delighted. He could move his head on his own!

A few times a day Nathan's right shoulder and arm would jerk rhythmically. This was the beginning of convulsions. The doctors prescribed Dilantin to help quiet this seizure activity. A direct injury to the brain may cause some of the brain cells to become overactive and set off a chain of events that produces a seizure. Sometimes children with brain damage have seizures for the rest of their lives. We were learning much about this complex organ called the brain. We were sad to think of the problems that could complicate Nathan's future: seizures, learning problems, paralysis, speech problems . . .

The nurses gave Nathan Valium, a strong nerve medicine, whenever they put the suction hose down his throat to draw the fluid from his windpipe. They did this every few hours, and it was uncomfortable for him. He got a lot of exercise with his left leg because he kicked during this time. The other leg wouldn't move. His right leg was growing thinner than his left one. Running dye through his veins proved that there weren't any blood clots in Nathan's leg, and the doctors concluded, as we had, that his right leg was growing thinner from lack of use.

We were facing another difficulty. The tube from the breathing machine can damage the throat if left in for too long. Dr. Minard explained the procedure for a tracheotomy. "We make a hole in the neck right above the collarbone that goes directly into the windpipe," he explained. "He also needs more nourishment than the IV can give him." I heartily agreed. I had noticed how thin he had become without eating for a week. "This looks long term, so we will perform a gastrostomy and insert a tube directly into his stomach to give him the food and vitamins he needs."

We gave our consent, and Dr. Minard made plans to do it the next day.

Nathan was becoming more alert to what was going on around him. But he also suffered more. If I could have suffered instead, I would have been glad. With everything he went through—blood draws, X-rays, or other tests—I found myself in my prayer closet again, suffering with Nathan. Many times I had to submit my will to God's anew. I knew I must be willing to undergo the suffering out of which character is born. He spoke to me through Psalm 138:3: "In the day when I cried thou answeredst me, and strengthenedst me with strength in my soul." I also felt the prayers of others from all over the country strengthening me. This song also became precious to me during this time:

> *I need the prayers of those I love,*
> *While trav'ling o'er life's rugged way,*
> *That I may true and faithful be,*
> *And live for Jesus ev'ry day.*
> *I want my friends to pray for me,*
> *To bear my tempted soul above,*
> *And intercede with God for me;*
> *I need the prayers of those I love.*

We kept getting calls and letters. One came from Susie Gilmore, a registered nurse from neighboring Vermont who occasionally came to our church. We had become friends shortly after we moved to New York. She offered to be Nathan's private-duty nurse whenever we needed it. "Free of charge," she assured us.

"Maybe God has something in this for us," Lloyd said thoughtfully, though neither of us knew how she could practice in our hospital since she was from another state.

We'd spent only a week in the hospital, but it seemed more like a month. Our feelings of dread and heaviness were giving way to excitement at Nathan's unusual signs of improvement. His eye was open all day, which gave us more time to stimulate his brain, trying to improve his mind and memory. Andy had given Nathan a big balloon. One side had a face printed on it. The other side was like a mirror. Nathan liked it. Lloyd untied it from the bedrail, pulled the balloon down within reach, and said, "Nathan, touch it." Nathan's left hand reached for it. He was uncoordinated, but it was his first effort to raise his hand by himself.

The sisters from church eased our children's burdens at home by taking turns bringing meals once a day. It was a beautiful picture of bearing one another's burdens. It made me think of the story of the blind man who met a lame man on a bad stretch of road. He asked the lame man to be kind enough to help him over the rough places. "I can't do it," said the lame man. "I'm not strong enough. I can hardly drag myself. But you are strong. If you carry me, I shall guide you, and we shall both be able to move along." So the blind man took the lame man on his back. One man used his strength; the other used his eyes. They soon passed the troublesome spot in the road. If we combine our forces, we can conquer life's troublesome places.

Another bright spot was a family friend, Sally Kurtz, who came from Pennsylvania. She used her managing ability to assist the children while we stayed at the hospital with Nathan. She pitched in with the work and filled a social need in their lives. The Bowman cousins also visited. And John, our Christian neighbor, often inspired us. One night as he and his wife Anna took our daughters, the Bowman cousins, and me home, we started to sing. I hadn't sung for such a long time, except quiet songs to Nathan. It felt so good to lift up my voice and let my emotions flow.

> *Oh, if you are sad and lonely,*
> *Life is but an empty tomb,*
> *Breathe a prayer to Jesus only,*
> *He will drive away the gloom.*
> *Jesus is the One.*
> *Yes, He's the only One.*
> *Let Him have His way*
> *Until the day is done;*
> *When He speaks you know,*
> *The clouds will have to go*
> *Just because He loves you so.[2]*

---

2. The words and music to this song are at the end of this book.

# 8.

# To Glorify Thee

*Call upon me in the day of trouble:*
*I will deliver thee,*
*and thou shalt glorify me.*
*— Psalm 50:15*

*C*ourage does not mean being unafraid. If we are not afraid, it is easy to do something. Real courage means being perfectly aware of the worst that can happen, being sick and entirely afraid, and yet not panicking or doing something wrong. That's how I felt the first time Dr. Percy, the pediatrician, talked to me about Nathan. It was only the third day. Not much recovery was noticeable yet.

"You do understand, Mrs. Martin?" he asked. "An injury like this always has some permanent, harmful effect on the patient."

Frightened tears sprang to my eyes. *Be not afraid, only believe.* This comforting promise attacked those fearful thoughts.

"A lot of people are praying," I said simply. The doctor came in, examined Nathan, and sat down. He exclaimed over

Nathan's progress. "You are a very strong family and a very strong person. I believe your God is answering your prayers."

"Jesus, my Saviour, gives inner strength and comfort. He's real in the lives of those who trust Him." I spoke with confidence. Those earlier fears had just dissolved. But we knew that without God's sustenance, we would go to pieces. So we answered with what came to us at the time and trusted God to help us express our faith so others might understand and be drawn closer to Him. And we did see people's hearts and minds being drawn to God through our experience.

Revelation 12:11 became meaningful to us: "They overcame him by the blood of the Lamb, and by the word of their testimony; and they loved not their lives unto the death." We had many opportunities to share our testimony with others. I read this thought in my devotional book one morning: "Be open and sensitive to every opportunity to communicate with another person. But remember it is God's responsibility to do the talking. You simply have to be available. He may want you to silently respond with a kind look or listen with a caring ear. He only needs an honest love that you will transmit from your soul."

I learned to love the song "To Glorify Thee."

> *Oh, may my life be to Thy praise, O Father.*
> *In all I do may Thou be magnified;*
> *Thou chosest me before the world's foundation,*
> *Thine own to be, that Thou be glorified.*
> *To glorify Thee, this is my plea;*
> *Work out Thy purpose, Thy plan for me.*

*A yielded vessel, Thine own to be;*
*Thy praise and glory, to live for Thee.*[3]

Our lives had changed drastically. For years I had been a homemaker with hardly an opportunity to meet people or share with others. I had greatly anticipated having children, but it had been almost frightening to look at our first baby and see her so tiny and helpless, so dependent. And there was no such thing as off-duty. What mother hasn't gone to bed almost too exhausted to sleep, only to have a sick child awaken her? There were always shoes and socks to find, faces and ears to wash, cuts and bruises to dress, wandering tots to be found, meals to be prepared, clothes to be laundered, tears to be kissed away, endless questions to be answered, and countless other things that required my time and energy to be focused on home.

Life at the pretzel bakery in a small town in Akron, Pennsylvania, offered a good opportunity to do more than make 1,200 pounds of pretzels a day. There was the daily responsibility of keeping relationships running smoothly between twelve employees, customers, distributors, and salesmen. After ten years of selling pretzels, a large farm was a drastic change, but a welcome one. Farm life was harder and not so prosperous, but we felt we were preparing our boys for a variety of occupations with all the different experiences a farm has to offer. Animals, machinery, nature, carpentry work, mechanical work, and all the daily jobs provided quite an education that they couldn't have gotten in town twisting pretzels every day. But our lives on the farm were largely separate from others.

3. The words to this song are at the end of this book.

Now we were thrust into a world of suffering people. We found ourselves sharing, listening, and identifying with their problems. They didn't need pity any more than we did. They needed genuine sympathy, support, and positive direction. We learned to know one family especially well when they faced the difficult decision of whether to keep their mother alive using machines or let her die. We were there for them when they finally gave the doctors permission to turn off the machines.

No two days were alike. One day's experience brought elation which the next day burst like a balloon pricked with a pin. Nathan's progress had a way of inspiring us to build up hope; then he would go through more tests and suffering that tried our faith.

The evening before Dr. Millard performed the tracheotomy and the gastrostomy, Lloyd discussed the procedure with Dr. Owen.

"There are two ways to perform a gastrostomy," Dr. Owen explained. "We can insert a permanent tube or a temporary one. With a permanent tube, it takes a minor surgical procedure to remove it. I think a temporary one will be sufficient in Nathan's case." We were glad for this less-invasive option.

The next day I was surprised to learn that Dr. Millard was planning on doing the permanent procedure after all. Dr. Owen had left it up to Dr. Millard's final judgment.

"A child can easily pull the temporary tube out and do more harm than good," Dr. Millard explained. But we wanted to keep things as simple as possible. I called home to Lloyd, who was as concerned as I was.

"Mary Ann, don't let him do it that way. Dr. Owen thought it was all right to put a temporary one in."

So I told the head nurse that we didn't want the doctor to do a permanent procedure on Nathan.

"Here they come to take him, Mrs. Martin," she said. "You'll have to go along down with them and speak to the doctor personally."

I was glad to walk down with the stretcher. Nathan wasn't frightened when they pushed him out of the room when I went along. I held his hand as we rode the elevator down to the operating room. We were escorted into a room full of workers wearing green uniforms and caps. With face masks on, they began immediately to prep Nathan. The anesthesiologists prepared to put him to sleep. I could feel everyone wondering what business I had down there.

Finally someone said, "He goes to the operating room," motioning to the huge sliding door to our right.

"May I speak to Dr. Millard?" I asked weakly.

He entered, clearly prepared to perform the operation. "Can I help you?"

"My husband wanted me to request a temporary gastrostomy. That's what he and Dr. Owen agreed on because that would eliminate another surgical procedure when it's time to take the tube out." My voice faltered as all eyes turned toward me.

"All right," he laughed, "I'll do it your way. But I'll put one stitch in it to secure it a little bit better, okay?"

"That's just fine," I said, thanking him as I left. Nathan was already fast asleep.

I spent the next few hours waiting anxiously. What was supposed to take an hour or two stretched into three hours, then four. Finally Nathan arrived back in the ICU. His strained, sad face relaxed when he saw me. I had not been allowed in the recovery room. I assumed that he had been crying in there, so I softly sang to him for a long time.

That evening when Lloyd came, I stayed a little longer than usual and visited with him. We prayed together before we parted. Then Nathan heard me ask Lloyd for the van key. Immediately his face showed all the expressions of crying. He knew I was going home. It tugged at my heart, but it pleased me that he understood what we were saying. Lloyd stepped closer to the bed and took his hand to reassure him.

Dr. Owen was concerned about the two main arteries through the neck. Another dye test determined that they were open, though partially restricted. But we and the doctors were glad to see blood flowing through them. If they had been closed, it would have meant no blood flow to the brain. Another cutdown was done. All the tubes and IVs were put on the other side. We were told that infection could set in if they stayed in the same place too long. Every day they did blood work on Nathan. Instead of sticking him every time, they just drew blood from a tiny valve.

I was anxious about the spinal tap. I had seen this procedure done ten years ago on someone else, and it had appeared to be a real ordeal. But the nurses said Nathan barely cringed. They found bacteria in the spinal fluid. My faith wasn't strong that night. I was tired, which made things look darker. I called home to tell them about the bacteria, which to me meant spinal meningitis. The children called Grandpa, and everyone was concerned about the serious, crippling illness. Nathan had been progressing so well.

We need not have worried, and when I came home from the hospital, I called Grandpa and told him the truth. The bacteria had cleared up easily with an antibiotic. We thanked God for this relief. The Lord gently rebuked and comforted me with Psalm 94:19: "In the multitude of my thoughts within me thy comforts delight my soul." In our relief, we worshiped Him with the same fervor we previously had pleaded to Him with.

Later that evening Justus and James asked, "Will Nathan ever walk again? Will he be normal? How long will he be in the hospital?"

I couldn't answer their questions, but it reassured them just to communicate their concerns. Justus was our quiet, dependable ten-year-old. His curly hair made him look different than our other boys. His work was always well done, and he was gentle, especially to his little brothers. At three and four years old, he had often led his brother James, who was two years younger, by the hand. James was eight years old now, with few words and a quick mind. His sober expression made it seem as if he weren't taking it in, but when he talked, it often brought a burst of laughter from the others. Justus and James cared for the calves and did the barn chores while Loyal and Victor took on the harder farm jobs.

June 7 had passed before we thought of our wedding anniversary. Lloyd and I had been married in a small Mennonite church. We had dated a few months when I was seventeen and he was nineteen, but we'd been too young and immature to find fulfillment in this friendship, so we had gone our individual ways for a while. Six years later, when I was twenty-three and Lloyd was twenty-five, we were married after a year of courtship. We were both Christians by then and had both taught school for a year. Now we reminisced about the promise we had made seventeen years ago for better or for worse.

# 9.

# Signs of Progress

*God is a refuge for us.*
*— Psalm 62:8*

$N$urses who were off-duty for a few days and returned were surprised at Nathan's progress. To us it seemed slow. He could squeeze my hand with his left hand and let go when I told him. The nurses called it responding on command. He still couldn't move his right side, but he did twitch when pinched. The doctors encouraged us to bring Nathan's favorite toys to the hospital. Seeing things he recognized and people he knew helped stimulate his mind.

Nathan enjoyed visits from his brothers best of all. We were surprised that the hospital allowed children to visit, even in a critically ill patient's room. The boys took turns coming in and staying for the whole day. It moved us to tears to see the left half of Nathan's face break into a bright smile. The right half remained paralyzed.

We showed him picture books and read Bible stories, *Wee Lamb* stories, and children's books. Nathan's favorite toy was a small yellow Tonka tractor his cousin Lois sent to him. He had just learned to use the fingers on his left hand, and they fit perfectly into the cab windows. He held it many of his waking hours, crying when it fell out of his hand. It came at the exact time it was needed most to encourage him to use his fingers and was excellent therapy.

One day Nathan's pediatrician visited. I told Nathan to put up one finger for Dr. Leister, then two fingers, then three, next four, and finally five. Nathan responded perfectly. Dr. Leister could hardly believe his eyes. "Baby!" he exclaimed in surprise. "That's wonderful! You are amazing!" He leaned over and kissed Nathan on the check.

We all continued to miss Nathan at home. Our lives were so different. Our days and nights at the hospital allowed only small slots of time for the things that needed to be done at home. The children accepted this temporary way of living, but when we thought of it dragging on for months, it looked tough. But we trusted that facing each day as it came and trusting our interrupted family life to God would have a maturing effect on our family.

Victor, at fourteen, was a great help around the farm. He kept the cows and the barn clean. He had outgrown his childhood allergies and was fast becoming strong and tall, just like his father's side of the family. He had a love for art and nature and was developing into a conscientious young man.

Between the company and the many phone calls, I tried to give some of my time to Joshua, who reached out his hands and cried whenever I came in the house. He had turned one in February and had brought much joy into our household. At his birth he'd looked like a healthy little boy with his round little head and his thick dark hair coming down over his ears. I immediately noticed tiny dents at the top of his ears that our other babies hadn't had, but I didn't think much of it. But within twenty minutes the doctor came in and said, "Lloyd, I think your baby is a Down syndrome child. We can't tell for sure. He will have to be tested."

I hardly believed him, but I examined our baby closely the next time they brought him to me. What with all the different theories bouncing back and forth, it was actually a relief to get the test results back verifying that our baby was indeed a Down syndrome child. In spite of our fears concerning him, he was our own little Joshua.

At first it had been difficult to think of him as "special." We gladly accepted and cared for him, but we felt the uncertainty of the future and the responsibility of giving him the best care possible. But we kept our worries about Joshua to ourselves, not even sharing them with our children.

Lloyd looked tired when I arrived at the hospital at 5:30 the next morning. He'd had a rough night. Nathan had been awake most of the night with much discomfort. Though we knew it was best not to keep Nathan drugged any more than necessary, it grieved us to see him in pain and discomfort. We continually turned to the Word of God for help during those times. Verses we had hardly noticed before came alive with meaning. As we drank them in, we felt refreshed, as though we were riding some inside track with our Lord as

He taught us deeper lessons about trust and dependence on Him. We loved the account of the Shepherd's voice in John 10. He guided us and gave us discernment as we read the Scriptures and prayed. His wonderful, powerful voice was deeper than the deepest pain in our hearts. "My flesh and my heart faileth: but God is the strength of my heart, and my portion for ever" (Psalm 73:26). "Thou shalt guide me with thy counsel, and afterward receive me to glory" (Psalm 73:24).

We often stopped to think about God letting Nathan live. We marveled at His love and praised Him. We didn't know the future and wondered what purpose God had for Nathan. The same day of his accident, another child his age was driven over and died shortly afterward. Later an eight-year-old from a family we knew was killed in a farm accident. We wondered why God took those children to Heaven and left Nathan in our keeping. All we could conclude was that Nathan's purpose here on earth was not fulfilled yet.

I once heard the walk of faith compared to traveling on an airplane. You never see the pilot or know his credentials, yet you step into that plane believing he is there and that he can handle the plane and the flight.

Friends and relatives sent money to help us pay the hospital bill. In one week the bill climbed to $20,000. The hospital wanted us to apply for financial assistance, but we had a principle not to accept insurance or public handouts to supply our needs, but to trust in God, who has promised to supply all our needs. We had seen Him do this often for others and knew He would do this for us. Our reaction to losing financial goods or security shows how much our hearts are deceived by the riches of this world.

June 10 dawned a beautiful spring day. A cool breeze, unusual for that time of year, invigorated me as I traced the familiar path from the parking area to the hospital entrance. Spring had come late this year. One visitor asked me how our garden was coming along. I had planted it before the accident, but had hardly thought of it since, so I replied honestly that I didn't know and didn't really care right then. The next day two families from our church weeded the garden and replanted the beans that had frozen in an unexpected late frost. Though I couldn't feel much interest in the garden at the time, I knew we would appreciate the harvest.

Many people asked if we were tired and how we passed the long hours. We hardly noticed our own inconveniences or discomforts, but focused on Nathan's. Most of our struggles were emotional. We bounced between the thrill of his progress and the desire for more progress. It still seemed unlikely that there wouldn't be serious permanent damage.

Nathan had rested very well the night before, so Lloyd had been able to get some sleep on the recliner beside Nathan's bed. During the day we noticed a partial opening of Nathan's left eye. Lloyd told him the story about the Good Samaritan. I asked Nathan about the story later, and he remembered quite a bit of it. That, too, was encouraging. We played with an ABC chart, and he pointed to the letters in his name. The nurses thought this was amazing. They had not thought he would be able to talk or learn, and now he could spell his name and was trying to talk to us. He would move his lips, though his breathing tube allowed no sound beyond a faint whisper. It was difficult to understand him, though sometimes I could. We both became frustrated easily when I couldn't. He was determined to make us understand him and would try until his frustration had him in tears. We tried to console him. Sometimes we just had to walk away until he forgot about it. His moods fluctuated a lot, which showed his emotional instability.

That evening the whole family visited, and he cried a lot. We knew we needed to keep him calm and help him rest, so we limited his visitors.

"What hurts?" I asked him.

"He can't point," Lloyd reminded me.

So I asked, "Does your head hurt?"

"No."

"Does your belly hurt?"

The answer was always yes. The pain sometimes became so severe that he threw himself over on his side with just the use of one leg.

"Don't you have anything to give him for his bellyache?" I asked the nurse one evening.

"No," she answered, "we really don't. You probably have a home remedy that would help as much as anything we have. He hasn't eaten anything for eleven days. His stomach is adjusting to the formula he is getting for nourishment."

This made me think. I had been depending fully on the doctors and nurses, but perhaps I could do more.

"He has been on strong antibiotics," I said to the nurse. "This took all the good bacteria out of his intestines. This is what gives him pain when his body tries to digest the formula."

"Yes," she agreed.

"Could we give him yogurt to help replace the bacteria that the antibiotics took out?"

"Yogurt he shall have." She marched right to the kitchen and brought back a cup of yogurt and a spoon. But we encountered another problem when I tried to feed it to him. He took the food into his mouth willingly enough, but when it got to the back of his mouth he looked frightened. He didn't know how to swallow.

He wanted the yogurt, so I kept trying and so did he. After a couple of days, he finally learned to swallow. But it went so slowly and he got so little of the yogurt that we both grew completely weary.

"This won't help." I expressed my discouragement to the nurse. "He barely gets a few teaspoons. And this processed yogurt doesn't have the bacteria he needs anyway. May I bring some homemade yogurt?" I asked doubtfully.

"You certainly may," she agreed.

I had learned to appreciate the thoughtfulness and cooperation of the nurses on Nathan's floor. "Could you put some into the gastrostomy tube?" I asked hopefully.

"We certainly will," she assured me.

From that day on, I brought homemade yogurt in cottage cheese containers. Each shift of nurses put a few tablespoons in with the formula that went through the tube directly into the stomach. The results were soon evident. His pain stopped. His food digested, and his bowel movements returned to normal.

Since Nathan was getting his fluids through his stomach, he didn't need the IV anymore, so it was removed. His left arm was free now, and he started to move it. It was poorly coordinated, but he got it to his nose, which he rubbed for a while. We hadn't known that his nose itched, or we would have gladly scratched it for him. It made us wonder if there are often little discomforts that could be remedied just as easily in other helpless invalids, if only we knew.

It also made me think how the nagging annoyances we face in life are often harder to bear than more traumatic experiences. The important thing is our reaction to them. God works with us every day, teaching us, molding us, shaping and smoothing the rough edges, making us more like Him. If we accept everything from His loving hands and thank Him for it, our lives can be wonderfully enriched by every problem and calamity that comes our way.

# 10.

# Healing Waters

*My people shall dwell in a peaceable habitation,*
*and in sure dwellings,*
*and in quiet resting places.*
— Isaiah 32:18

*T*he nurses were giving me more responsibility for Nathan's care. They disconnected the tubes and brought a basin, soap, and towels. I bathed him, brushed his teeth, and combed his hair. Now that the bandages were off his head, we could see that his hair had been shaved in front.

I had always enjoyed nursing and had pursued that occupation before I was married. I had worked as a ward clerk on a medical floor for two years and taken the proper schooling. But the nursing supervisor had answered "no" emphatically when I asked about wearing my prayer veiling. "The nurse's cap can take its place. It is far more substantial than your thin cap," she replied.

But I wore the prayer veiling as a sign of submission to God's headship order. The nurse's cap would only identify me as a nurse. I'd had other concerns about entering a professional field and eventually decided this was not the field for me. I told a friend, "I really believe God wants to use me for service somehow. I don't know how exactly, but I want to give myself to God and allow Him to use me in every opportunity I meet in life." Life itself is a school. The experiences we face are the lessons; the trials are the tests. God is our instructor.

As the years went by and I considered our family of nine children, I thought of nursing their hurts, cuts, stomachaches, and illnesses, of giving remedies, vitamins, and prescriptions, and I concluded that I was a nurse after all, and it was fulfilling.

We had tried to teach Nathan modesty, to not dress and undress in public, to close the bathroom door, and to try to be neatly dressed with his shirt tucked in and pants not too tight. Now, with his ingrained concepts of modesty, he became upset when the nurses bathed him or uncovered him. He didn't realize that there were exceptions.

After I bathed Nathan, I sat on the large recliner with Nathan on my lap. The nurses reconnected the tubes and oxygen and said I could hold him for an hour or two. Many visitors were moved to tears to see him out of bed. "It was almost like seeing him rise from the dead," someone said. It was wonderful to be able to hold him after nearly two weeks. He showed his contentment by his expression. Nathan was emotionally unstable and cried very easily, which made us even more determined to support him. He had not had a difficult babyhood, but he had experienced more trauma in the past two weeks than some experience in a lifetime. Not only did he endure the suffering and the frustrations of being paralyzed, but also the sudden change from all he had ever known. His stable home life was now altered to having only one parent at alternate times. And it looked like our fractured family life would go on for a long time—perhaps forever in Nathan's eyes.

We had the choice to sink into self-pity or rise to the life of faith. Each of our children sensed his responsibilities and the importance of keeping the home functioning. Keturah showed me a verse that comforted her from Jeremiah 31:28. "This sounds like Nathan, Mom," she said, and read, "So will I watch over them, to build, and to plant, saith the LORD." Building is gradual, and it takes things a while to grow when they are planted. It spoke to her of Nathan's gradual restoration.

I meditated on Ezekiel 47 and was impressed with those healing waters. This Scripture may have been for Israel, but those healing waters seemed to me a very real experience for Nathan. He was gradually improving beyond the doctor's highest expectations. The waters in the story issued out of the altar. The altar meant a sacrifice and a complete yielding of the will. Then those blessed waters flowed. First just to the ankles, then to the knees. They rose until one had to swim to cross. Everything these waters came in contact with received life, healing, and restoration. Its fish were a consolation to the poor fisherman. The desert it came in contact with flourished. The trees grew and became strong. The leaves were used for medicine and didn't fade. The fruit was food for everyone.

Our prayer was that God would restore Nathan so thoroughly with the healing waters that flowed from the promises of His Word that Nathan could be a blessing and a useful person in a variety of ways to all he came in contact with, and that the Lord's healing waters would continue to flow in him throughout his life.

"Here, you may have a popsicle," the nurse said kindly as she presented Nathan with the red, icy treat. He held it with his left hand and licked it. After biting a piece off and not being able to swallow it, he gave it back to me, moving his lips to say, "I don't want the popsicle." I held it in my hand where he could see it. Typical of little boys, in a short time he reached for it again.

After two weeks, Nathan was eating again, though apple-sauce and orange juice were about all the nourishment he got besides his yogurt-formula feeding.

The new tracheotomy tube Dr. Minard put in Nathan's neck was more convenient than the first breathing tube. I watched as they pulled the one out of the hole in his neck and inserted another one that could be disconnected. When Nathan was connected to the breathing machine, it did all the work. When disconnected, he had to breathe on his own. Then he could make sounds from his throat. His voice was very quiet. But after not hearing him talk for two weeks, it was a real thrill to hear his dear voice again.

After one of Allen and Sadie's regular visits, Nathan said weakly, "I'm going to get well because Allen prayed for me." Allen was a great entertainer, and Nathan loved his visits. Sometimes Allen brought a homemade card from their children or a story. One time it was a bulldozer game, which kept Nathan's attention for a long time. The game was a box with a clear plastic top. Inside were bridges, sawdust, and background scenery with roads. The sawdust could be plowed into piles by moving a magnet on the bottom of the box. Nathan gained coordination in his left hand as he made the bulldozer go under bridges and plow roads. As his left hand improved, he increased movement all over his left side. His right side remained motionless.

My herb cupboard was almost a joke around our home. One of my hobbies was learning the medicinal value of different herbs and herbal combinations. My family had benefited from my hobby from time to time. Now I wondered if I couldn't help Nathan.

The professional staff gave Nathan the drugs they thought were best. We were thankful for their medical abilities and techniques. Still, I wondered if Nathan might benefit from some herbs, such as a good spasmodic mixture to calm his nerves. Maybe then he wouldn't need as much Valium. I also had some calming herb drops for the stomach to aid his digestion and some good multivitamin drops. I talked to the nurses about it, and they agreed that I could try them.

Apparently this was put in the nurses' notes, because the doctor asked me about it. I was pleased to show him the herb combination. "Is it all right to give these to Nathan?" I asked him.

He didn't answer for a while as he studied the ingredients. "Oh, I guess so," he laughed. "They may not help him, but they won't hurt him either."

Dr. Perry, Nathan's pediatrician, came to see him again. I told Nathan to count for the doctor. I wanted the doctor to see that Nathan could talk and that his mind was functioning. He very readily counted to ten for the doctor. "My five-year-old can't do that! Your prayers really work." He added seriously,

"I'm very impressed. Do you know what? When we face another difficult experience with someone else, I may call upon you to pray for them and the situation. Is that all right with you?"

"Dr. Perry," I said soberly, "I'm going to take that seriously. Yes, you certainly may do that."

Sure enough, a few weeks later when I called to inquire about one of our other children's illnesses, he came to the telephone and said, "Mrs. Martin, we are facing a very difficult condition right now. Remember this request in prayer, would you?"

"I certainly will, Doctor. God answers prayer." I never knew what it was or the results, but I believe God received glory from the incident in His own way.

# *11.*

# God's Redeemed Children

*Not redeemed with corruptible things,*
*as silver and gold,*
*but with the precious blood of Christ.*
— *1 Peter 1:18, 19*

*O*ne of the greatest comforts to a suffering individual is the presence of a loving, understanding, supportive companion. Just knowing the person is there is adequate even when words are few.

Nathan had slept very well the last few nights, so we left him alone one night. Uncle Aaron and Aunt Leona were visiting from Pennsylvania. Uncle Aaron stayed at the hospital with Lloyd and Nathan until about midnight. When Nathan was sound asleep, they both came home. It was the first night we had left him alone in the excellent care of the nurses. Despite their professionalism and kindness, we knew that Nathan, in his insecurity, needed the security and comfort of people he knew and loved. Our family was his secure world.

Nathan was crying when I came in at five o'clock the next morning. The nurses had done everything they could to console him. Finally they had given him a nerve medicine to quiet him, but he felt forsaken. Before, when and if he woke up, Lloyd was there—perhaps sound asleep, but still there.

Nathan complained of a headache. He was so upset I could hardly console him. Finally he said, "Mama, I want to go home with you."

"We won't go home again and leave you here alone," I promised Nathan. He believed me, but he didn't forget this incident for a long time. Even months later, he would refer to "the night Papa left me alone." Maybe we had sheltered him too much in his five years. We never pushed our children out in public among strangers to make them tough or bold. Shyness among strangers can help protect a child. The personal responsibility to be sociable and independent can come gradually with maturity.

Jesus will never leave us nor forsake us (Hebrews 13:5). Nathan felt forsaken when we went home without him. We thought about that and discussed it. When we are in the midst of distressing, frustrating, or fearful situations, our heavenly Father gives the redeemed child of God the greatest source of encouragement and strength. Many times we are comforted or strengthened simply by being reminded in the Word of God of His presence. The words, "Lo, I am with you," put the fearful heart to rest and motivate the weak to be strong. This experience with Nathan clinched in our minds that the presence of a loving father is a comfort to a son in distress.

Nathan had progressed enough to be given his own room. We liked the pleasant atmosphere and increased privacy of the pediatric ward. Nathan was unhooked from all but the feeding and oxygen tubes. He breathed on his own most of the time.

Nathan said good-bye to the ICU nurses, who fussed about missing him and insisted that he come back and visit them soon. I tried to explain to him that he was going to a different part of the hospital where it was nicer. But he had to adjust to new nurses who had different methods. He cried and wanted to go back to the ICU. Later he told me he didn't like the new bed because it looked like a crib.

As we pushed the stretcher out of the ICU's double doors, we left behind two weeks of experiences. Nathan would never remember being there or most of what happened while he was there. He did remember the move to the pediatric ward. He was made comfortable in a beautiful room with a huge low window. From his bed, he had a panoramic view of the city. Fascinating pictures adorned the walls. The nurses placed a cot in the room for us to sleep on. Nathan was given a small wheelchair. Several church groups, including our own, started sunshine boxes. Someone collected an item or two from each family in the church, wrapped them, and put them in a decorated box. Each day Nathan opened one of the packages. The nurses were fascinated and asked every day what he had opened. This bright spot in his day helped dispel some of the monotony of his shut-in routine. It gave us all something to look forward to.

Every small gift brought sunshine, but the gift Nathan cherished most while he was in the hospital was a bubblegum machine. He wasn't allowed to eat any because it would be dangerous if it were to get stuck in his throat, but it brought so much enjoyment to Nathan as he shared some with everyone who came. He wanted me to keep pennies lying on his beside stand so he could put one in the plastic machine and make a little round piece of bubblegum roll out.

When his brothers came in, he talked and talked to them. His whispers sounded like music to us, who had wondered if he would ever talk again.

Sally was Dr. Owen's nurse. He only took time to see critically ill patients. She made rounds every day and was the go-between for the patient and Dr. Owen. Nathan liked her sweet, gentle, expressive ways very much. She was definitely his favorite. She hugged and kissed him sometimes when she came in to see him.

"Don't feed me so fast. Don't put so much on the spoon."

I was used to feeding babies. Nathan had more preferences. The nurses left it up to me to order whatever I wanted him to eat, even if it wasn't on the menu. He cleaned up everything I fed him. In between meals, he ate Cheerios, yogurt, or ice cream.

I had more time at home after we started a third shift. Our church friends had offered to relieve us at the hospital, but we had felt that only family could give Nathan the security he needed while he was critically ill. Susanna, Lloyd's youngest sister and a favorite aunt of our children, came up to help us for a week. Grandma came along with her. Susanna was always like one of our family. When we had lived at the bakery, she and Grandma had lived in a house Lloyd had built on the other side of the paved driveway. During the trying, difficult years when the children were small, I often felt overwhelmed. Susanna was a great help and relieved me many times. She was willing to help with the garden work, cleaning, canning, or whatever the project was. She seemed to know just the right moment to drop in and lend a helping hand. The children have many precious memories of Susanna taking them for walks so I could have a quiet hour. She was also a faithful standby at the bakery, and she demonstrated a character which made her a good example for our girls. "When we get big we want to be like Aunt Susanna," they often said.

Lloyd's mother was a genuine mother to me. I could never relate to those with in-law problems. My stepmother had died of heart failure when I was a teenager, so I always turned to Lloyd's mother to teach me how to can fruit or blanch vegetables. She taught me much about being economical and caring for sick children. Grandma also filled a supportive role for others around the bakery who were not in her family.

We were told that stroke victims take a year and a half to recover, so we knew Nathan needed a long time yet for the damaged area of his brain to heal. After a few days in the pediatric ward, he could move his head right and left and his left side freely. He began the long, hard journey through physical therapy. First the therapist came to his room. Now we had something constructive to do with our time at the hospital. We exercised his feet by helping him "run," pushing both feet back and forth in unison with our hands. His brain had forgotten that he had a right side, so it couldn't give a command to move his right side. So his left hand had to teach it. We made him use his left hand to take hold of his right hand and bring it up to his nose or to our noses or wherever we told him. The left hand was sending messages to the brain to help the brain relearn how to make the right side move.

We took Nathan down to the hospital basement for more physical therapy. He hated this. But it amazed us how quickly he was relearning everything. First he had to learn to roll over like a new baby. Then he had to learn to crawl, which was very frustrating for him.

We took him on wheelchair rides. The sitting position hurt his head. His equilibrium was off. Everything floated in front of his eyes, and he became sick to his stomach. We just took short walks at first. Each day we went a little farther. The playroom was a big attraction, but soon he wanted to go back to his room.

"Mom, I can hear the GMC. It's Papa! No, wait, it's just a truck on the road." There were lots of traffic noises, but Nathan always recognized the sound of the GMC. I was pleased that he remembered how it sounded.

"Do you remember the tractors we have at home on the farm?"

He told me about the Ford, the Massey, and the White. As far as we could tell, he remembered everything from before the accident. We praised the Lord for this.

"Do you remember going along out in the field to pick up stones?"

"Oh, yes," he spoke up quickly. "Loyal brought a big one to the scoop."

"Do you remember falling off the tractor?" I spoke gently. I hated to bring up the subject, but I felt like we needed to know if he remembered.

"No." He shook his head slowly. "Maybe I fell asleep."

Maybe he did. At any rate, I was glad he didn't have any memory of that moment.

The third Sunday forenoon was dreary. Times when I knew others were in church had a tendency to get a little long. Nathan and I did some therapy and played with a bead number game from the playroom. From the comfortable armchair I sat in, I could look across the city street. The houses looked drab on this cloudy day. The vehicles jostled noisily on the street below. I readjusted Nathan's body to a more comfortable position and started singing. It helped lift my spirit and calmed him.

"They sang that song in my grandmother's church."

We were startled to see a lad of about eleven sitting in a wheelchair in the doorway.

"Did you like that?" I asked.

"Oh, yes," he immediately said. "I like to hear you sing. Could you sing some more?"

"I suppose I could. What would you like me to sing?"

He didn't care. I spent the rest of the forenoon entertaining both boys with singing.

Nathan fell asleep. Talkative, lonely Jason had many questions and many things to tell me because I had time to listen and was willing. He told me about his unfortunate home. I talked to him about Heaven, Jesus, and told him some Bible stories. From that day on, I talked with Jason daily.

"When I get big I'm going to be a preacher," he stated firmly one day.

Jason had suffered a lot of pain from burns on his legs. Our older boys met Jason and became good friends with him. They made a scrapbook for him to help pass his lonely hours. We prayed for him, committing his young life into God's care. We prayed that some seed of truth would be sown in his heart during the time we spent with him that would give him a desire to make the right choice in life—life in Christ—the only right choice.

# 12.

# A Light to the World

*Let not your heart be troubled,*
*neither let it be afraid.*
*— John 14:27*

Nathan dreaded the sight of the large, blue rubber mat in the basement therapy room. When we saw how difficult it was to stand him on his feet, old fears arose in our hearts. The old fears said, "He'll never be normal. He'll never walk again." The doctors were becoming more and more optimistic, which gave us renewed hope. The Lord continued to bless us with inspiring verses when we needed them most. We wondered how people made it through traumatic experiences without the comforting presence of the Lord.

JoAnne, Nathan's therapist, explained to us, "He can now roll both ways and get on his knees, but he doesn't have any balance and becomes limp like a rag when he tries to stand.

The good part of Nathan's mind will have to teach the damaged part to use the limbs it has forgotten are there."

Nathan had lost eight pounds during the beginning of his hospital stay, but he was starting to gain some of it back. The nurses could hardly believe that he asked for a bowl of Cheerios after he finished his Cream of Wheat and egg.

"He sure doesn't need that gastrostomy tube the doctor ordered with the way he eats." So cheerful, plump Mrs. Kline came scurrying into the room to take "that contraption" out.

"May I watch?" I asked eagerly.

"Sure," she answered. The nurses tried to slowly pull the tube out of Nathan's belly. It should have slid right out, but it wouldn't. They read and reread the directions and tried again.

"Dr. Millard said he was going to put a stitch inside so that it wouldn't come out so easily," I mentioned.

The nurses seemed perplexed. They called the doctor, who pulled on the tube until the stitches were visible, snipped the stitches, and slid the tube right out. The oxygen tube was next. This too the doctor pulled out very simply. He pushed the holes in Nathan's stomach and neck back together.

"No stitches?" I asked.

"No. It heals just like that. But when Nathan coughs he must use his hand to put pressure on the gauze over the opening, or the air will come out the hole in his neck instead of his nose and mouth."

It was much easier for Nathan to talk after this, and it seemed as though he wanted to make up for lost time. He talked and talked. There were no more tubes attached to him. We were all delighted.

We were beginning to think about taking Nathan home. What would the doctor say to that?

"Nathan is very helpless," he answered.

We then told him about our friend from Vermont, the registered nurse who had offered private duty assistance if we needed it. Dr. Owen thought that would be a satisfactory arrangement and said he would let Nathan go home in three days if she was living with us to observe Nathan and be there in case anything serious happened. We had been told to expect another couple of months in the hospital, so this was very welcome news.

Nathan's attitude and expression were brighter. He was more enthusiastic than he had been since he was in the hospital. He almost shouted into the phone to Keturah, "I'm coming home in three days!"

As eager as we were for this transition, the unknown future looked difficult with his helpless condition. Could we properly care for our invalid child at home? My thoughts were drawn to God and the contentment of being in His love and will. This time I was encouraged in a different way rather than through a special verse. During the twenty-five mile-drive to the hospital at daybreak the next morning, I had a breathtaking experience that drew my heart and soul heavenward in worship to God, the maker of all things. I felt that this particular morning had been especially planned for my inspiration, encouragement, and blessing.

The night before I had been home alone with the children. The thunder crashed and the lightning flashed as the rain came down in torrents. A storm helps us sense our own helplessness and teaches us to depend on God for safety. Though we trust God completely to keep us from harm, even the strongest Christian is relieved when the storm ceases. Spiritual storms affect us the same way. They threaten to overthrow our spiritual lives, but once weathered, they bring strength and maturity to the soul. So the calm morning after the stormy night held double meaning for me on this morning. The golden warmth of the June sun flooded the landscape and reflected off woodland trees framed against the dark green shades of evergreens. The countryside looked exceptionally refreshed by the night's rains.

Suddenly I noticed two bright, colorful rainbows arched across the western sky. Then two graceful creatures leaped out of the underbrush into the clearing ahead and bounded onto the road in front of me. I slowed and watched the pair leaping gracefully along the side of the road just ahead of me. Then, with a leap and a bound, the deer disappeared into the dense woods ahead. Songs of praise burst spontaneously from my lips the rest of the way to the hospital.

Nathan was awake and talking to Lloyd when I arrived.

"My face feels funny, Papa."

"How does it feel, son?" Lloyd made Nathan comfortable on his lap in the big armchair.

"It feels like little things crawling all over the side that I can't move very much."

"Is that right?" Lloyd laughed. "That's Jesus healing you."

"When God heals, it tickles." Nathan smiled and partially raised his right hand. Physical therapy was doing wonders for him. Almost daily there were improvements in his movement. We continued to work with him between appointments. We held his knees together and mildly applied pressure. Then he tried to pull them apart himself with his leg muscles. We also practiced bicycling motions every day.

Nurses from other floors, visitors, and other hospital staff stopped in to see Nathan. They chatted, asked questions, or shared thoughts about faith, God, and prayer. Many times we thought of David's prayer the first night Nathan was admitted to the hospital: "May this be an experience that astonishes even the doctors and nurses so they will marvel at Your miraculous healing power." This was happening.

We kept asking ourselves if we were learning what God wanted to teach us. Our lives are the only Bible many, many people read. If love and thankfulness to God are not there, all the other ingredients are meaningless.

During our last checkup with Dr. Millard, he said emphatically, "I want to tell you, Mrs. Martin, this has been one of the most memorable experiences I have ever had in my professional practice as a doctor. In fact, I would say the very *most* memorable." He paused. "When I looked at Nathan's X-rays for the first time, I was sure he would not leave the hospital alive. The X-rays showed the skull shattered like an eggshell the complete circumference of his head. It's a miracle, is all I can say!"

Each doctor in his turn made a similar statement.

The countdown continued. Nathan didn't forget. Two nights and one day to go. He talked about climbing trees and riding bikes. He talked about playing with his beloved brothers. It did my heart good just to hear him. His enthusiasm helped lessen my concern about the future. We needed constant grace and kept committing Nathan's future to God. Sometimes we momentarily wavered in our faith. God reminded us of His promises to us and gently rebuked us with Luke 24:38: "Why are ye troubled? and why do thoughts arise in your hearts?" God was proving to be all that we trusted Him to be, and He was fulfilling the promises we received from His Word the night of the accident.

We were constantly overwhelmed with God's love and closeness when we trusted Him. That's how I had felt when Jesus first came into my heart. I had been troubled and felt so sinful and unable to cope with all the adjustments of being a teenager. I had been trying to live a Christian life for a long time and felt defeated. Finally in desperation I went on my knees beside my bed. "O God," I groaned. "I can't leave this room until I find peace—some relief from this terrible turmoil within." I had often prayed before, but this time it was different. The Holy Spirit helped me confess every sinful inclination and wrong tendency in my life. He showed me how to commit myself wholly and unreservedly to loving God, who had sent His Son, Jesus, to shed His blood to wash away my sins. Something wonderful happened in my soul. The new birth is really unexplainable. Jesus likened it to the wind. We can't see it, but we see what is happening to the trees as the wind blows through them. And we certainly can feel it. The difficult circumstances were still in my life, but they didn't matter anymore. My God had everything in control and would work it all out for His own good.

During the weeks of suffering with Nathan, this thought often consoled me. This peace that passeth all understanding was all I really wanted in my life.

One evening I was compelled to escape to my room and pray earnestly. This sudden awareness of danger made me feel troubled and restless. "Am I developing a phobia of accidents because of Nathan's accident?" I didn't know, but committed each one of the family to God, praying for each person's safety and for His protection over us. A load was lifted, and I felt assurance in my soul that all would be well. A short time later, I learned that a heavy bale of hay had been thrown down one of the hay holes in the barn from high up in the haymow. It landed on Lloyd's head, knocking him over. His head was cut on a water bowl, but he wasn't hurt in any other way. We were overwhelmed with the way God protects us, especially after we heard that this happened to someone else around the same time, severing a vertebra and leaving him paralyzed.

Life "is even a vapor, that appeareth for a little time, and then vanisheth away" (James 4:14).

This crisis with Nathan had made me so dependent on God that I sensed His guidance in all areas, even urging me to pray and guiding my prayers. The experience was also helping me understand my own weaknesses. Through my failures, I was learning not to rely on my own strength, but to lean upon God and His great strength, trusting in Him.

# 13.

# A Red-Letter Day

*In your patience*
*possess ye your souls.*
*— Luke 21:19*

If I made the calendars and chose which important dates to make red-letter days, June 20 would undoubtedly be one of them. That was the day Lloyd and I brought Nathan home from the hospital. His three-week stay was brief compared to the two or three months we had expected, but it had seemed a long wait. It took patience even after the discharge was written up.

"It sure takes longer to leave the hospital than it does to come in," Lloyd said as we waited on the last detailed instructions from the doctor and collected the Dilantin prescription.

Nathan thought he was going home and was very tired. We first had to go to the other hospital in town by ambulance for a professional hearing test before we could finally head home. The test showed that Nathan had extensive hearing loss in his right ear. His left ear still had a fair amount of hearing ability. We had often interpreted for the doctors because Nathan couldn't understand what they were saying.

The nurses wrote parting notes to us and to Nathan.

*Nathan,*

*You are a very special young man. All of us in ICU are extremely happy you have done so well so fast. Watching the love and care your family shares has been very rewarding to many of us—reminded us of the "good part" of our job. We wish you all of life's best, and we would enjoy very much if you would stop in to see us every once in a while.*

*Sincerely,*
*Judy*

*Nathan,*

*My name is Eliza and I have enjoyed taking care of you and meeting your family, but best of all I am so glad that you are better. Keep making progress and come see us for a visit when you are well.*

*— Eliza*

*Nathan,*

*Best of everything on your road to recovery. I hope you do as well as you have here. You certainly are one of the cutest boys we've had! Good luck with your progress. I'm sure your brothers can't wait for you to get home to help with the chores. See you hopefully when you're up and about.*

*— Len*

*Nathan,*

*I'm so glad you are doing well. You're so lucky to have caring and loving family and friends who visit you. I pray you continue to get better. Please come and visit us. God bless you.*

*— Martha*

These dear people meant a lot to us, both for the care they gave Nathan and the kindness they showed us.

Before we arrived home, the children had great fun preparing to celebrate Nathan's homecoming. The girls had baked a cake and decorated it with names, lots of designs, and candy. "Welcome home" signs were tacked on the walls, and colorful balloons were strung across the room. Best of all was the low table in the corner of the room with the gifts Nathan had opened so far from the five sunshine boxes. The unopened gifts were attractively arranged in their decorated boxes in the corner of the room. Nathan was delighted.

A cousin, Cindy, was with the children when we arrived with Nathan. What a joyous welcome home! Everyone wanted to be with Nathan, especially James. Nathan's brothers were all very willing and supportive. Before the accident, the boys had sometimes considered Nathan a tagalong, since he was smaller and couldn't keep up. Now everyone was more than willing to do all they could for him.

Lloyd gathered the family together for prayer before we went to bed. Each of us prayed, thanking God for Nathan and praying for his continued recovery.

We made a bed downstairs with a three-inch foam-rubber mattress pad with egg-shaped air pockets designed for the comfort of patients who are in bed most of the time. It helped prevent bedsores and stiffness. In the daytime there was usually someone on Nathan's bed playing with him or entertaining him. At night it wasn't hard to get someone to sleep with him, as everyone wanted his turn. We had to say no to our younger children, as whoever was "on duty" needed to be able to get drinks for Nathan or help him to the bathroom.

Susie Gilmore had come the evening before and was with us during Nathan's discharge. She stayed for almost a week. She proved to be a very pleasant nurse to have in our home. Susie changed the dressing on Nathan's neck opening, gave him his medicine, and helped us make decisions concerning Nathan's welfare. We all tried to watch him carefully.

As our family routine settled back in, we turned our attention to teaching Nathan how to walk. Three days a week he went to physical therapy. This dreaded ordeal usually brought tears. The therapy wasn't that hard, but he hated going back to the hospital. We determined to be loving and patient with him, but we had to be firm also. "Don't cry, Nathan. Be brave," we would say before we left. "We'll get a cheeseburger at Burger King when it's over." On treatment days, we also let him open an extra gift from the sunshine box.

These treatments took only an hour. With coaxing and encouragement, Nathan usually got hold of himself before we arrived at the hospital. It was always a relief to him if Jerry was the therapist. JoAnne was the head therapist and was very nice, but Nathan's first few sessions had been very painful, and he associated them with her. Sometimes it may be more comfortable to stay in a crippled condition than to launch out with the discipline and effort to get well. Nathan felt we were trying to make him do things he couldn't do.

Susie, our faithful nurse, always insisted on washing the dishes. With our large family, we probably washed more dishes in a week than she did in a year. But our evening dishwashing was a time of fellowship.

A few days after Nathan came home, he was propped with pillows on the couch in the kitchen so that he didn't have to be alone in the living room. We had determined to watch him all the time to be sure he didn't bump his head. But this night we grew careless. When we heard the bump, we all dropped our towels, dishes, and brooms and rushed to Nathan. He had tried to get off the couch alone. Even though he was learning to use his hands and feet, he had no normal reflexes to protect himself when falling. We watched him for signs of a concussion and observed his pupils. He seemed all right. It was a good sign that he was trying things by himself, even though he could have been hurt.

Within a week of coming home, Nathan could crawl on his hands and knees. Sometimes his right hand, which was very weak, would buckle, and then he'd fall on his head with a bang. It gave us a real scare whenever his head, tender yet from the accident, hit the floor. After a few terrifying bumps, we bought a motorcycle helmet to protect his head from injury and give us peace of mind. He wore it when he tried to walk or get around on his own.

One day he lay on his bed, looking out the window with a troubled expression. "Mama," he said softly, "I thought when I came home from the hospital I'd be better."

"You are getting better," I explained. "God is healing you."

"But I thought I could climb trees like I used to do."

"Yes, Nathan, I trust that you can someday. You thought that in the hospital you were sick, but at home you'd be immediately better and could do everything you did before. But you must be patient and wait until God heals you. You must try hard, and that will help you get better faster."

"Am I a cripple?" was the next question.

"You are crippled now because you can't walk. But someday I'm sure you will walk again."

Nathan needed much reassurance as the days went by. We told him that people who are crippled on earth are not crippled in Heaven. Jesus gives them brand-new bodies. He liked it when we sang "Hallelujah Square," especially one verse:

*Now I saw a cripple, dragging his feet,*
*He couldn't walk as we do down the street;*
*I said, "My friend, I feel sorry for you,"*
*But he said, "Up in Heaven I'm gonna walk just like you."*
*I'll see all my friends in Hallelujah Square,*
*What a wonderful time we'll all have up there;*
*We'll sing and praise Jesus, His glory to share,*
*And you'll not see one cripple in Hallelujah Square.*

Neighbors and friends often stopped in to visit us and to see Nathan. As soon as he'd wake up in the morning, he would ask, "Mama, who's coming today?" His friend Tim from church, who was his age, came and spent a whole afternoon with Nathan. His friends helped him try to kick a ball. While they held it, he tried to kick it out of their hands. With their encouragement, he got better and better at it. We also helped him practice catching the ball.

Nathan's left side was coordinated enough that he could feed himself with that hand. We were thankful that Nathan could do as much as he was able to.

Our neighbor John and his son Johnnie walked over almost every day. "What can you do today?" John would ask.

Nathan made small, noticeable improvements every day, and he gladly showed John what he could do.

Samuel continued his visits. One time Nathan told Samuel that he loved him. Samuel was so touched that he broke down in tears.

The road back to health still required patience on Nathan's part and ours. God wasn't finished teaching us lessons from this school of experience yet. He wanted to conquer more areas in our life and bring us to complete surrender to His will. Christian graces do not come by chance. As we are willing to go through what He sends our way, the peaceable fruits of righteousness are blessed results.

* * *

"Mama, it's raining outside." Nathan's sparkling blue eyes looked sincerely from his wheelchair to where I was busy in the kitchen.

"Are you sure?" I looked up in surprise and glanced at the early morning sun gleaming in the kitchen window.

"Yes, I can hear it raining," he persisted.

"Oh, I see," I said thoughtfully. "I think your ears are playing tricks on you. There is fluid behind your eardrum yet. That's what you hear. It's not really raining," I explained.

Nathan stared soberly out the window for a long time. The fluid from his brain wasn't leaking out his ears or nose as before, but was evaporating behind the eardrum. It would still be a couple of months before that healed completely.

Nathan kept gaining weight and loved to be dressed in trousers and shirt instead of his pajamas. As long as we looked at his progress, we were encouraged. But whenever we looked at what he still had to learn, it looked discouraging.

The gift table was filling up. Puzzles, teddies, wind-up and battery toys, coloring books, trucks . . . He treasured his little flashlight. He usually went for the biggest package first. "The nicest gifts don't always come in the biggest packages," Lloyd had told Nathan when he had opened this gift. The Jungle Express and the cylinder truck were among his favorite toys. He unselfishly shared his gifts with his brothers. "This is all yours," we told him, "but we all belong together, so your brothers can play with them too." Our company generally paid attention to Micah too. It was hard for our three-year-old to see his brother open a gift every day and not get anything for himself.

Sometimes it seemed like we had three babies. Joshua really was the baby. Nathan needed attention like a baby. And Micah's insecurity from feeling neglected made him act like one. When he clung to us, we usually took him up in our laps, wondering if this was how children felt when their mothers dropped them off at the baby sitter's to go to work. Did those children ever find the security they would have known with Mama being there? Micah was sandwiched between Nathan, who got a lot of attention now because of the accident, and Joshua, our Down syndrome child. We needed to be sure to give Micah as much attention as our needier children.

One day we took Joshua for his routine screening at the local rehabilitation center. They evaluated his progress and tested his abilities according to his age and offered us encouragement on how we could give him the proper stimulation. We took Micah along this time to enjoy the children there and see all the toys and activities. We watched the children enjoying the swimming pool.

When we came home, I drew Micah onto my lap and asked, "What did you like best today?"

His large brown eyes looked innocently into mine. "They just like Joshua," he said slowly. And I realized that, again, another child had been the focus of everyone's attention. In Micah's young eyes, that meant they liked Joshua and not him. I held him and talked to him until he squirmed from my lap, reassured of at least his mother's love.

Micah, too, had had problems when he was born. He hadn't breathed for the first five minutes of his life. I had known something was wrong because the nurses hadn't given him to me the whole first day. "Your baby is weak," was all they would say. The doctor was quite blunt a few hours later. "Your baby is on a monitor that keeps a close watch on his breathing and heartbeat. He turns blue and stops breathing. He has been having seizures. The lack of oxygen to his brain has caused brain damage. He very likely has cerebral palsy. This condition affects the center of the brain which deals with muscular control."

The ministers from our church were granted permission to go into the nursery after sufficiently scrubbing their hands and donning hospital gowns. They laid hands on Micah's head and prayed, asking for healing for his damaged mind and committing him to God.

A week later he was still having difficulties, but we brought him home from the hospital on phenobarbital, a drug that controls and prevents seizures. A technician taught us artificial respiration and how to use the monitor. Electrodes were fastened to Micah's chest and run to a machine. An alarm would go off if he stopped breathing, alerting us to administer artificial respiration. But we never had to. We gradually took him off the medication, and in two months we sent the monitor back. We decided to trust God and were greatly blessed to watch a perfectly normal baby develop and blossom into good health and vitality. He walked at nine months. We attributed Micah's miraculous development to prayer.

Now we had another miracle child.

Remembering Micah's babyhood and how handicapped he could have been often helped me to be patient through his innocent childish misbehavior—like when he brought sand in on the kitchen floor, or crawled into a bathtub with a few inches of water after we dressed him in his good clothes for company. Sure, there were times when our children needed discipline. We had to discern between innocent misdeeds and the stubborn, selfish, inborn nature of a child which must be brought into subjection with the rod. But a good sense of humor at innocent, childish pranks went a long way when we were tired and our children were mischievous.

# 14.

# Nights of Terror

*For every one that asketh receiveth.*
*If his son ask bread, will he give him a stone?*
*— Matthew 7:8, 9*

*J*ust as parents delight in each step their baby takes, we delighted in every new achievement of Nathan's. He spent much of his time on the couch in the kitchen. First he pulled himself up to a sitting position; then he stood so he could look out the window. His hearing had shown some improvement, but we still had to speak loudly and often repeat what we had said. We gradually took him off the Dilantin and gave him calming herbs for his nerves. Seizures never made their ugly appearance. We praised God for His mercy and healing power in this. In every step of progress, waiting patiently was an important tick in the perfect timing of God's clock. We found strength in trusting and waiting on His timing.

We began working on fine motor skills. Every day we encouraged Nathan to color one picture. We also had him write his name, first with his left hand and then with his right. He had learned to eat, write, and color with his left hand while his right side was paralyzed. Now we were working on both sides. His writing with the right hand was barely legible at first, but every day showed a little improvement. Whenever we went to a doctor for physical therapy, he took a paper along with his name written on it to show how he was doing. They were amazed at his progress.

He still had a long way to go. Proper brain stimulation taught him to do the things he had known how to do before. He learned to take small steps if we steadied his trunk, though he still struggled with balance. We helped him stand and kept him as steady as possible. Then we let him go and caught him as he fell. By July 1 he was able to walk while we held one arm. We didn't have to support his body anymore.

A child loves to run, so it wasn't a surprise to us when Nathan announced, "I want to run."

"All right," Keturah said. "You run." She supported him under his arms as he put forth the effort. It didn't go too well, but he found some satisfaction in trying.

His color improved as he spent more time in the sunshine. Nathan could go anywhere on his hands and knees. If we couldn't find him, we needed only to look out in the pea patch. He loved to sit in the garden and eat raw peas. Opening the pea pods was great therapy for his underdeveloped fine motor skills, and the peas were good for him too.

"Nathan, come play with us in the sandbox," his brothers would often say. This too was inexpensive but valuable therapy. In the sunshine with his favorite sunglasses on, he spent many hours developing coordination by using a shovel and other sandbox toys.

I tucked Nathan under the covers one evening as usual. It was nice to have the little boys sleeping together again. Nathan had stopped insisting on having an older brother sleep with him. The boys had just enjoyed the story about Jacob's dream of a ladder going all the way up to Heaven and angels ascending and descending on the ladder. This story fascinated the little boys, and they started asking questions about Heaven. It was hard to describe the beauty and reality of Heaven when I hadn't seen it myself, but I did my best.

"I want to go to Heaven," Micah concluded emphatically after my description.

Nathan looked at him very soberly and exclaimed, "But, Micah, you have to die first!"

Death seemed very real to Nathan.

"Not everyone will die," I explained. "This is what we are looking for." Then we talked of Jesus coming to take us home.

One of the greatest gifts we can give to our children is knowledge of the Bible. Its stories are a foundation on which to build all the truths and principles of God's Word. We often sang the children's song, "The wise man built his house upon a rock, and the rains came tumbling down." The floods came, but they could not shake the house because it was built upon a rock. We taught them that the Word of God gives this foundation to our lives. "But the foolish man built his house upon the sand." The same stormy environment made this house come tumbling down. We explained that this is what happens when we build our lives on worldly wisdom. It's not as much fun in reality when the house on the sand goes *crash* as it is for a child to sing about it and clap his hands to show the crash. The story of brave David killing the bear and later the giant, Daniel in the lions' den, Noah and the Flood, and Jonah swallowed by the whale were some of our children's favorites. We knew these stories were building a vital foundation of Bible knowledge and encouraging good character. "That from a child thou hast known the holy scriptures, which are able to make thee wise unto salvation" (2 Timothy 3:15).

Lloyd and I woke with a start later that evening. "Whatever is wrong?" Another scream of terror filled the night air. We made a dash for the little boys' room. I took Nathan in my arms. "What's wrong, Nathan?" We shook him gently to awaken him. I could feel his sweaty forehead as he grasped my neck.

"I was falling off a cliff," he sobbed softly on my shoulder.

"You're all right, Nathan. It was just a dream." We tried to console our quivering son. "You're right here in your bedroom with your brothers."

After a drink, prayer, and much reassurance, we tucked him back in bed. We wondered how long these nightmares would last. This wasn't the first night we had rushed to his side when his screams pierced the night. The night before he had been drowning in deep water. Before that a ferocious animal had been tearing him to pieces. We often carried him to our bed for the rest of the night.

We began to pray and to request the prayers of others for healing for Nathan's emotions. He didn't remember everything he had gone through in the hospital, but the subconscious experience was very real to him, and it wasn't letting him forget. It takes more than just physical healing to restore a person to complete health. Scars in the subconscious mind cause emotional trauma that disturbs or hinders the emotional development of a child or an adult for years. We knew that only Jesus could reach into the most complex center of his nervous system and take away the fears. So we committed him to God's care again, trusting in His mercy.

That was the last terrifying dream Nathan had.

Thinking of all the suffering in the world made us sad. The terror, trauma, and scars left by broken homes or severe illnesses cause emotional damage to children who don't fully understand what's happening. Someone who is close to a suffering child can give support. Left to himself with this insecurity, he could be crippled emotionally or mentally for life.

Loving grandparents give a child much stability. Nathan couldn't remember Grandpa's earlier visit, so he was excited when we told him Grandpa was coming again.

"How many times must I sleep before Grandpa comes?" he asked us daily for a week. Finally the day came. We don't know who got the most satisfaction, Nathan or Grandpa, as they paged through the five scrapbooks Nathan had received as gifts from various congregations. Each person had filled a page with pictures, art, inspirational thoughts, poems, or other things they thought might amuse Nathan.

Grandpa was Nathan's constant companion. He had always been a great help to our small children. Many times he rocked and sang them to sleep, singing from memory songs he had learned long ago. We knew these times were as fulfilling to

Grandpa as they were to the children. We often thought of the Book of Ruth, in which Naomi was told that Ruth's child would be "a nourisher of thine old age." We thought sadly of elderly folks in nursing homes who miss out on the blessings and fulfillment of associating freely with children and adults of all ages.

Nathan started to enjoy his tricycle in the barn. We soon learned that it was very important for him to wear his helmet in there. His tumbles could be quite hard, but his reflexes were improving, and he put out his hands to break his falls. The tricycle exercise was good for him, but the falls were scary. High-top shoes gave his ankles strong support and helped him walk and keep his balance.

Since we weren't going to the hospital so often anymore, we had more time to do other things. One evening we sat down and read the letters and cards that had come the first few weeks. They had meant a lot to us when we read them in our hurry. But now they meant even more to us as we took the time to read and meditate on all the encouragements and truths from thoughtful Christians.

Many deeds continued to bring cheer and encouragement and prevent despondent moments. Every day a card shaped like an apple came in the mail with nice verses on it, along with "An apple a day keeps the doctor away." It was fun to guess who was sending them until the last one revealed the sender's name. "For the laid-up one" cards came in the mail for seven days, the last one revealing the thoughtful person's name. Then it was "The Good Samaritan" who daily deposited homemade cards in the shapes of animals with verses, songs, and sayings.

They arrived in almost any unexpected way, sent always by "The Good Samaritan." They might come through a neighbor, a friend, or we might find one under a rock on the porch. The last one revealed our neighbors as the makers. Even our tractor mechanic brought seven baby ducklings as a gift for Nathan. The children all enjoyed these black ducklings immensely, though the ducklings didn't enjoy us. We kept them penned up for a while, but they soon made their escape. These thoughtful gifts brightened our days and helped lift our discouragement.

# 15.
# Concluding Blessings

*He healeth the broken in heart,*
*and bindeth up their wounds.*
*— Psalm 147:3*

"*I* was glad when they said unto me, Let us go into the house of the Lord."

July 14 was a comfortably warm summer day in New York, and the children's voices sang joyously in our family van as we rode to church together.

Nathan had to be steadied with one hand as he walked into the church house. The children enjoyed leading him around. Samuel announced Nathan's presence, and the whole congregation rejoiced to see our boy, who had been so near death, back in church. Our heavenly Father had bound up the wounds so skillfully that few scars remained on any of us. We hardly remembered the crushing hurt. We mostly felt excitement and joy at his rapid healing. Our hearts were overwhelmed with praise to God, who had accomplished it all.

Lloyd had devotions in church that day. He spoke of Nathan's recovery and progress, thanking everyone for their prayers, the meals brought in, the visits, gifts, and all the favors done for us during this time.

It was my first time back in church as well. It was so good to sit under the sound of the Gospel again.

Come Monday, it was back to the hospital for a visit. We walked through the familiar doors of the ICU to visit the nurses. Sally, Dr. Owen's helper, was making her rounds. She lifted Nathan up in her arms and hugged him. The nurses all gathered around to see him and talk to him.

"Oh, look how well he's doing!" they all exclaimed. "See how he can walk! Amazing! It's a miracle!"

The head nurse's eyes grew moist as she expressed sincere delight in his marvelous recovery. But Nathan wanted to get out of there as soon as possible. The attention made him nervous. He didn't remember most of them. The psychological healing in his subconscious mind was going to take time.

By August we only went back for physical therapy once a week. He practiced going up steps, playing ball, and catching, kicking, and throwing the ball first with the left side and then with the right. Then they worked on fine motor skills. Large floor puzzles, rings he had to lift to put on pegs, and writing all helped redevelop the skills he'd once had.

We still had to see two doctors—Dr. Hillerman, the ear specialist, and every three months Dr. Owen.

"Those ears were plumb full of blood when I first saw them," Dr. Owen said. "The right eardrum looks very good. There is no visible damage, but it doesn't have much hearing because of some nerve damage. The left eardrum was severely damaged in the accident, but his hearing is fairly good. The bones were fractured in both ears. Only time will tell if more nerve endings will come together again and improve his hearing."

The good news was that there was no liquid behind his eardrums anymore. We had suspected that, because Nathan didn't hear it raining anymore in the morning.

Dr. Hillerman had another concern. "I don't like what I see. The left eardrum is caving in over the bone. This will cause more hearing loss and problems with infections," he said soberly. "We don't want that to happen. We should perform an operation in the near future to insert a plastic tube in the eardrum to let air in. This will extend the eardrum out where it belongs and keep it dry behind it. Shall we schedule it for two weeks from today?"

"Yes," we quickly agreed.

We didn't tell Nathan right away. We thought we would wait until it was closer to time for him to be admitted to the hospital. We didn't want him to worry unnecessarily, but we wanted him properly prepared and to know what was going to happen to him. The unknown always caused him more uncertainty and fear.

As the day approached, we prepared him as best we knew how. "You will only have to stay one day," we explained. It still was unnerving to him. Again many prayers went up to God's throne on his behalf.

Soon the day came for Nathan's pre-operation test. This operation didn't look quite as serious to us as the three operations doctors had expected to perform on Nathan's head. Those had been miraculously avoided. This time, we were fully resigned to having it done.

At the pre-operation examination, Dr. Hillerman took out his flashlight. He shone it in Nathan's ear, paused a moment, and shone it again.

"I don't believe this," he proclaimed in excited surprise. "This just doesn't happen. Mr. and Mrs. Martin," he said in response to our questioning looks, "your son doesn't need an operation after all. That eardrum is where it belongs."

"Praise the Lord!" Lloyd and I reverently acknowledged God's power in unison.

"I can't understand this," Dr. Hillerman continued. "Someone must have prayed. Things like this don't just happen."

"We did pray," Lloyd replied. "In fact, our whole church did."

"You must have had the right words." The doctor smiled, still shaking his head in disbelief.

"God answers the prayer of faith," Lloyd replied. "It's not the words we use."

"Dr. Hillerman," I said, "sometimes I've seen Nathan holding his nose shut and pinching his mouth closed. Then he blows until his face gets red. I asked him one day why he was doing that, and he told me it made his ears feel better."

"Amazing!"

I never saw a doctor so excited.

"Dr. Bowman!" he called to the other doctor in the hall. "This little fellow is brilliant! He had a collapsed eardrum and learned how to blow it out without anyone teaching him how to do it. Extraordinary!"

We gave God all the glory. He knows all things and knows how to inspire us to do that which brings about the results He wants.

We praised and glorified God on our way home, where we shared with the rest of the family the wonderful news of God's great mercy and healing power.

This was the fourth planned operation we had escaped. The fourth mountain cast into the sea. The next time we saw Dr. Hillerman, the nurse exclaimed with emotion, "Here comes the miracle boy! It gives me a funny feeling inside every time I see him."

We were often reminded of the healing waters that brought the gradual healing we had read about in Ezekiel. We rejoiced to see the effects of the waters slowly conquering and healing Nathan's body and mind.

"Children are amazing," Dr. Owen had told us. "They recuperate a whole lot more readily than adults do."

August 10, Nathan ran across the lawn to his brothers all by himself. His gait was unsteady, and at times he fell, but he persevered.

"I'm six today! I'm six today!" he shouted gleefully. "I'm old enough to go to school!"

We had planned on letting him go to school that fall, but that had been before the accident. Now we wondered. We asked, and the doctor gave his permission. We sought God's direction and decided that another year at home would give him a chance to more fully recuperate physically, mentally, and emotionally.

It brought tears to Nathan's eyes when he saw the others going to school that September without him.

The neurologist showed us a series of exercises to help Nathan's mind relate properly to his limbs. He had to crawl, touching his knees with his hands as he crawled. He also did marching exercises and many other exercises which helped him not to drag his right foot and helped his knees to function properly. He bounced a balloon above his head to encourage his eyes to work together. He had twenty-twenty vision in each eye, but some muscles were pinched, which prevented them from working together. By now he was able to eat and write well with his right hand.

The past months seemed like a dream. Our renewed love and closeness to God reminded us that we had gone through a trial. Our basic beliefs hadn't changed, but our priorities had. The things of eternal value seemed much, much more important to all of us. It takes self-denial not to crowd God out into the fringes of our lives. Although this had never been our intention, we felt we might have been doing just that before Nathan's accident. But walking through the crisis together had refreshed us spiritually and made us determined to stay even closer to God than we had been before. God had helped us to see our needs and fall on our knees before Him.

The experience brought forth much good fruit from the children too. Three of our children gave their hearts to God within a year after the accident—first Victor, then Hannah, then Loyal. This brought great joy to our hearts. If we could see all the good that comes through suffering, we might not fight it so, but by faith understand that God's mercy is enough. No matter how rough the road, a heart that is open toward God will see His mercy and kindness along the way. It was through His mercy that Nathan did not have more permanent damage. It was through His mercy that the accident happened when it did, during a time when we weren't busy with haying or planting or harvest. The whole healing process was a speedy, merciful experience. All this helped us to see God's hand and to seek His guidance and will for us even more. This, too, was His mercy.

"O satisfy us early with thy mercy; that we may rejoice and be glad all our days" (Psalm 90:14).

# *Epilogue*

# A Beautiful Benediction

*For length of days, and long life,*
*and peace, shall they add to thee.*
*— Proverbs 3:2*

"Report card time again." I gladly accepted the report cards my young scholars handed me as they came trooping in the door. "I hope you did your best," I encouraged each one.

"We appreciate all your hard work at school," I continued as I examined each report. I paused when I came to Nathan's. All As and Bs. I smiled my approval. I recalled the doctor's words of seven years before . . . "brain damage . . . never learn . . . never talk."

"Thank you, God," I whispered.

Nathan had recovered far beyond our expectations. His gradual but complete healing had brought many emotional moments and many challenges. He'd fallen many times, but with a laugh he was soon up and on his way.

"Nathan, come race to the tree," a school chum had boasted mischievously upon Nathan's arrival back at school. Boys will be boys, and all boys like to win a race. Others soon teased Nathan into contests he couldn't win.

"Son, we must all accept ourselves as we are," I admonished. "We all have our weak points and strong points. To be an athlete or the fastest runner in the school is not what God values most in a boy, but to be strong in faith and spirit. Such strength comes from being courageous through difficult experiences. We can't pity ourselves when we are treated unjustly. You have an opportunity to learn these lessons young in life," I tried to explain lovingly.

"Yes," agreed Lloyd. "You must pray for the boys. They don't mean to be unkind; they just don't think about how you must feel. I'm sure their parents will talk with them. Just be thankful you can run, climb, and play. At one time the doctor said you would never be able to. You have progressed immensely."

The boys' friendship soon knit and matured, and they accepted Nathan with his slight handicap.

"How long will it take these hearing aids to make my ears better?"

I was startled by the serious question coming from my then six-year-old. I paused to think before explaining. "You see, Nathan, Loyal, and Hannah wear glasses because their eyes need them to help them see better. Just like that, your ears need aid to help you hear better. You will probably always need them."

Nathan nodded and walked away thoughtfully. But after that he no longer seemed concerned about his hearing aids.

"We continue to marvel, Mrs. Martin," Dr. Hillerman emphasized during one of Nathan's annual checkups. "That pocket in his ear we have been watching for the last five years is doing unusually well. They occasionally get infected and mastoids develop, but no such thing for this boy. And that eye that was angled outward from a pinched nerve has straightened out beautifully. He is focusing normally now. This sure is a lucky case."

"It's more than luck, Dr. Hillerman," I spoke confidently. "It's God."

Dr. Hillerman turned toward the door to see his next patient. "You have me convinced," he said, glancing back at Nathan.

Occasional visits to a neurologist and continued physical therapy completed Nathan's recovery.

A year after Nathan's accident, we had welcomed a new member into our family. This blond-haired, blue-eyed boy did not at all resemble his father, but he was our eighth son, and I told Lloyd, "Surely one must be your namesake." Lloyd consented, and so Lloyd Andrew became a beautiful benediction to our home. Not only had God spared the life of our injured son, He had blessed our home with another beautiful, healthy baby. Not only had God answered our prayers for healing and life, He had added and multiplied our blessings. We praised God for his liberal gifts and prayed that the ripples of these blessings would flow from our home to others in our school, in our community, and in other communities.

* * *

"Do you remember me?" I heard a familiar voice while grocery shopping.

"Oh, yes! You're one of the nurses from the intensive care unit."

I gave her a brief update on Nathan's progress. Nathan had lost hearing in one ear and had to wear a hearing aid in the other, and a slight weakness on his right side was noticeable when he walked or ran, but other than that he had recovered completely.

"Mrs. Martin," the nurse said, "we have had other trauma patients similar to Nathan. We encouraged them and ourselves with the fact that since Nathan recovered, this patient can too. But," she added seriously, "they don't recover like he did."

Our hearts were continually refreshed with God's mercy toward us. We focused our attention not on our miraculously-healed son, but on our heavenly Father's great love. We had learned that when we trust that mercy completely in hard experiences, they usually aren't as hard as they appear. The worst that could happen to His Son, He turned into the best that could happen for the world. Even so, we trusted that the worst that could happen to us would turn out to be the best for developing faith, godliness, and submission to His will.

# To Glorify Thee

*Oh, may my life be to Thy praise, O Father.*
*In all I do may Thou be magnified;*
*Thou chosest me before the world's foundation,*
*Thine own to be, that Thou be glorified.*

*CHORUS:*
*To glorify Thee, this is my plea;*
*Work out Thy purpose, Thy plan for me.*
*A yielded vessel, Thine own to be;*
*Thy praise and glory, to live for Thee.*

*Oh, may my life be to Thy praise, O Saviour.*
*Thy finished work in all Thy glory see.*
*Oh, precious thought that Thou entrusted to me*
*This task to praise and glorify Thee.*

*Oh, may my life be to Thy praise, O Spirit.*
*This temple filled, empowered, and yielded be,*
*That in Thy strength my life may glorify Thee*
*In life or death, in all Thou hast for me.*

# A Christian Home

Barbara B. Hart, 1916

Jean Sibelius, 1865-1957

1. O give us homes built firm up-on the Sav-iour,
Where Christ is head and coun-se-lor and guide;
Where ev'-ry child is taught His love and fa-vor
And gives his heart to Christ, the cru-ci-fied.
How sweet to know that though his foot-steps wa-ver,
His faith-ful Lord is work-ing by His side!

2. O give us homes with god-ly fa-thers, moth-ers,
Who al-ways place their hope and trust in Him;
Whose ten-der pa-tience tur-moil nev-er both-ers,
Whose calm and cour-age trou-ble can-not dim;
A home where each finds joy in serv-ing oth-ers,
And love still shines, tho' days be dark and grim.

3. O give us homes where Christ is Lord and Mas-ter,
The Bi-ble read, the pre-cious hymns still sung;
Where prayer comes first in peace or in dis-as-ter,
Their bonds of love no en-e-my can sev-er;
And praise is nat-ural speech to ev'-ry tongue;
Where moun-tains move be-fore a faith that's vas-ter,
And Christ suf-fi-cient is for old and young.

4. O Lord, our God, our homes are Thine for-ev-er!
We trust to Thee their prob-lems, toil, and care;
If Thou art al-ways Lord and Mas-ter there:
Be Thou the cen-ter of our least en-dea-vor
Be Thou our Guest, our hearts and homes to share.

# Jesus Is the One

Adger M. Pace

Gertie Rast

1. When the day is dark be - fore you, And the clouds are hang - ing low,
2. Oh, if you are sad and lone - ly, Life is but an emp - ty tomb,
3. When you come to cross the riv - er, He will be your Friend and guide;

There is one who watch - es o'er you, Ev - 'ry where that you may go.
Breathe a prayer to Je - sus on - ly, He will drive a - way the gloom.
You can live with Him for - ev - er, O - ver on the oth - er side.

*Chorus:*

Je - sus is the One, yes, He's the on - ly One, Let Him have His

way un - til the day is done; When He speaks you know, the

clouds will have to go, Just be - cause He loves you so, loves you so.

Christian Light Publications, Inc., is a nonprofit, conservative Mennonite publishing company providing Christ-centered, Biblical literature including books, Gospel tracts, Sunday school materials, summer Bible school materials, and a full curriculum for Christian day schools and homeschools. Though produced primarily in English, some books, tracts, and school materials are also available in Spanish.

For more information about the ministry of CLP or its publications, or for spiritual help, please contact us at:

Christian Light Publications, Inc.
P. O. Box 1212
Harrisonburg, VA 22803-1212

Telephone—540-434-0768
Fax—540-433-8896
E-mail—info@clp.org
www.clp.org